Jolt

*Shake up your thinking and upgrade
your impact for extraordinary success*

Richard Tyler

CAPSTONE
A Wiley Brand

This edition first published 2015
© 2015 Richard Tyler

Registered office
John Wiley and Sons Ltd, The Atrium, Southern Gate, Chichester, West Sussex, PO19
8SQ, United Kingdom

For details of our global editorial offices, for customer services and for information about
how to apply for permission to reuse the copyright material in this book please see our
website at www.wiley.com.

The right of the author to be identified as the author of this work has been asserted in
accordance with the Copyright, Designs and Patents Act 1988.

Wiley publishes in a variety of print and electronic formats and by print-on-demand. Some
material included with standard print versions of this book may not be included in e-books or
in print-on-demand. If this book refers to media such as a CD or DVD that is not included in
the version you purchased, you may download this material at http://booksupport.wiley.com.
For more information about Wiley products, visit www.wiley.com.

Designations used by companies to distinguish their products are often claimed as
trademarks. All brand names and product names used in this book and on its cover are trade
names, service marks, trademarks or registered trademarks of their respective owners. The
publisher and the book are not associated with any product or vendor mentioned in this
book. None of the companies referenced within the book have endorsed the book.

Limit of Liability/Disclaimer of Warranty: While the publisher and author have used their
best efforts in preparing this book, they make no representations or warranties with
respect to the accuracy or completeness of the contents of this book and specifically
disclaim any implied warranties of merchantability or fitness for a particular purpose. It
is sold on the understanding that the publisher is not engaged in rendering professional
services and neither the publisher nor the author shall be liable for damages arising
herefrom. If professional advice or other expert assistance is required, the services of a
competent professional should be sought.

Library of Congress Cataloging-in-Publication Data

Tyler, Richard, 1972-
    Jolt : shake up your thinking and upgrade your impact for extraordinary
success / Richard Tyler.
      pages cm
    Includes index.
    ISBN 978-0-85708-598-6 (pbk.)
    1. Change (Psychology)   2. Organizational change.   3. Success. I. Title.
    BF637.C4T95 2015
    158–dc23
                                                                    2014047601
A catalogue record for this book is available from the British Library.

ISBN 978-0-857-08598-6 (pbk)
ISBN 978-0-857-08599-3 (ebk)   ISBN 978-0-857-08600-6 (ebk)

Cover Design & Illustration: Kathy Davis/Wiley

Set in 10/15pt and Frutiger LT Std by Aptara
Printed in Great Britain by TJ International Ltd, Padstow, Cornwall, UK

'*Jolt* upgrades you from "happy, safe and fine" to "extraordinary, fearless and outstanding". An exciting, exhilarating, and empowering journey.'
Elizabeth L Kuhnke, Bestselling author, conference speaker and executive coach

'Richard Tyler once told tone deaf me that everyone can learn to sing. I now know it to be true. In my case I also learned to play the music, handbuild the instrument from raw materials – my beautiful electric guitar – and write the song. Oh yes, and along the way I chose, aged 59, to move on from a successful career as an academic, a Surgeon and a Chief Executive and create my own independent business. Truly there are no limits; it just took a Jolt from Tyler to get started.'
Dr Mark Goldman, Surgeon, Former NHS Chief Executive and Director of the Goldman Partnership

'Steve Jobs didn't take Apple into the stratosphere by emulating IBM, but by thinking radically different. How we find those triggers and build on those key blocks to make us achieve extraordinary action is the mission of *Jolt*. Richard gives some building blocks where we can identify what we need to do to make step changes in our performance and that of others. High levels of success only come from stepping out of our comfort zone and taking on challenges that may ordinarily scare us, but learning how and where the markers are can help. Massive changes are not needed. If one of two parallel railways has a one degree shift, 50 miles later they are a mile apart. Keep one degree shifts emerging in your culture and dramatic change takes shape.'
Ian Dormer CDir FIoD, Chairman, Institute of Directors

'Are you up for the challenge? Through practical experiences, supported by evidence-based theories, Richard challenges assumptions and mental models. You can't fail to be impressed by the simplification of robust theories and personal experience, which together help the reader define, or even redefine, who they are and who they want to be. *Jolt* is a great leadership journey... be open; be honest; be ambitious and you will be jolted.'
Theresa Nelson, Chief Officer for Workforce Development at Birmingham Children's Hospital – *Passionate about developing people and creating great organizations through leadership*

'As the speed of change accelerates, it is essential that bigger companies like BBC Worldwide continually shake up the accepted way of doing things. Jolting our thinking is no longer a luxury. It is essential for survival and growth.'
Tim Davie, CEO, BBC Worldwide

'Irrespective of where you are in the pecking order, none of us can afford to sit back and become complacent. The current unprecedented pace of change and challenges to accepted wisdom mean that we all need to continuously upgrade and reinvent ourselves – and use every bit of talent and courage in the process. Richard delivers this message loud and clear through *Jolt*! If you are ready for some fresh thinking and a new perspective, then I suggest you get stuck into your own copy of *Jolt* – then watch the changes go viral (and watch out – there may be horror and some drama on the way to the happy ending!)'
Etay Katz, Partner, Allen & Overy LLP – *Etay takes an active role in mentoring lawyers through their development stages and in shaping the firm's training programme designed for its emerging talents*

'A cognitive *Jolt* to transform your business and your life.'
Dave Coplin, Chief Envisioning Officer, Microsoft UK

'At Innocent, we look to disrupt the norms and lead the way. For this to happen, we have to *Jolt*!'
Richard Reed, co-founder Innocent

'This book contains some great insights to help disrupt you and your business out of "auto mortgage payment" and ensure your hardware (brain) is getting its vital upgrades. Unlike your phone it's got to last a lifetime – give it a *Jolt*!'
James Gentle, Innovations Marketing Manager, KP Snacks

For all those that have Jolted me on the journey so far. Thank you.

Contents

Introduction

With ordinary talent and extraordinary perseverance, all things are attainable.

Thomas Foxwell Buxton

This book will Jolt you. Not for the shock factor, but because the challenges faced by anyone in a leadership position are immense and in this new age there needs to be a better way to make an impact. Too many are busy 'doing', yet are not actually being productive. People are working longer hours than ever before, yet in that time, how significantly are they really transforming and innovating their space?

The luxury of just being 'good' and remaining a leader are gone and the consequences of failing to Jolt are severe – take Blockbusters, Jessops, Comet – why did they collapse? They stayed comfortable. They didn't disrupt. They failed to lead.

On the flipside, look at Apple, Innocent, Dyson, Amazon – they are successful because they push at the edges and do dare to disrupt the industry standards.

Don't be fooled into thinking you are safe. If you are not shaking up your industry now, someone else will be.

You, like me, will recognize that the world is moving at an extraordinary pace. Probably faster than ever before and the one thing we can be sure of going forward, is that the pace will only continue to accelerate. There was a time however, where you could pretty much be 'good' and feel 'safe' as a leader by predicting what you delivered last week, last month and even last year, would continue to be a success. 'Let's keep churning out the same as it's worked for us before!' Well those days have passed us by. Business schools focused on metrics, measurables and the bottom line. Case studies, reports and spreadsheets ruled!

The space we are in now has shifted beyond recognition and the expectation of what has to be delivered has multiplied. We can no longer rely on telling the story where leaders scrape by with knowledge alone, technical competency and a textbook approach – the world is ready and, in most cases, demanding something more. The requirement now is for organizations and their leaders to be led away from pure process, out-of-date habits and mediocrity and towards a hunger for embracing something extraordinary where the outcome is to transform and not just fix.

The ability to transform, however, requires so much more than simple technical knowledge. While that is important, it is only a small part of the story; courage, listening, noticing, intuition, improvisation and engaging others in transformation is the larger part. In your role as a leader today, *it is not just about playing the notes well, but listening to what's emerging in the spaces in-between.*

That final statement is key. A good musician will be competent at playing the notes and lots of them together. The same is true for many *good* leaders, they will also be capable of playing many notes and lots of them together. What differs for the *extraordinary* musicians is that they are the ones that stop and listen to the spaces in between the notes. This is the moment that becomes their choice point for creating an extraordinary narrative and ensuring it finds its way to landing with their audience. It is the moment when they hold the questions:

What am I noticing?

How can I build on this?

What can I do to deepen my listening?

How can I become even more of a contribution?

When did you last ask yourself the same questions?

> It is not just about playing the notes well, but listening to what's emerging in the spaces in-between.

In the business space we currently operate within, playing the notes is simply no longer enough: reliance upon *banging out as many notes as you can* is a high risk strategy that most cannot afford to take. Yet, still, many organizations continue to focus on developing only the behaviours and skills that fit with the 'old story' – where the number of notes played in a day was the measure of success. It has all changed – the audience is now demanding that we deliver a more relevant and up-to-date story.

Just recently I read in the paper that John Cridland, director-general of the CBI, has written a hard-hitting report recommending that schools and the government pay far greater attention to developing the attitude and character of children while in education. The past and current focus is on exam results; more knowledge, more learning and more tick boxes, yet employers believe that an agile mind, emotional intelligence and the desire to go the extra mile are most important. Skills are much easier to instill if the attitude to learn and upgrade yourself is in place.

Here's the thing – much of what you do already works well. It must or you wouldn't have got this far in life. The question for you though is this: will it be enough to take you beyond where you are now in order that you can play with extraordinary?

> The attitude and behaviours that made you good will not be the same ones that make you extraordinary – doing more of the same will not unleash your success.

Ideas spread

Over the past 15 years, I have worked across the globe as a consultant and coach to some of the world's biggest organizations, helping them to *Jolt* their own thinking. Jolting them to be bold and to start embracing this new world. Shaking up their thinking and the action that they take. Offering them a new lens to look through. Encouraging them to dare more.

Cajoling them to make new choices rather than play out old habits simply because '*it did work that way once... in 1874.'*

In simple terms, provoking them to adopt a more *Artful* approach, thereby creating the choice to elevate towards something extraordinary.

Having witnessed my clients now begin to exceed their audience's expectations, have happier people amongst their workforce and generate more extraordinary moments than ordinary ones, I think that it is now the time for the Jolt to ripple further. I want this thinking to go viral. I want to start a revolution where more people can begin to flirt with extraordinary. The route to that exists here, through Jolt!

This is **your** Jolt. Like anything worth having though, it is good to share it with others. I ask you to pass this Jolt on. Jolt yourself. Jolt your team. Jolt your manager. Jolt your culture. Doing all this will in turn Jolt your audience, meaning that you remain on their radar for all the right reasons.

An Artful approach

During your life, at some point and in some way, you will have been touched by the arts; a play, a piece of dance, a song, an orchestra, a singer, an actor or actress, a film, a painting … it will have moved you. It will have created a connection and provoked a response. It will have been extraordinary. It will have offered you a Jolt!

Now take a moment to consider what it might have been that made it so extraordinary for you.

What was it about the performer?

How was it they connected with you?

What did it Jolt you from and to?

What made the difference between that experience being an ordinary one and an extraordinary one?

I frequently ask these questions of my clients and, without exception, each one has admitted a profound effect when they experienced extraordinary performers sharing an extraordinary performance. When I enquire about what it was that made the difference between ordinary and extraordinary, there is rarely any mention of 'the great voice' or some superhuman skill set they possessed. The answers are pretty consistent; the courage to dare, the bravery, passion, energy, commitment, a well rehearsed talent, connection, a vision, listening to the audience, precise communication and a personal accountability for the success of the performance.

The world of the arts offers a unique framework for building even greater possibilities and presents you with a new lens to look through: a lens that invites both its performers and its audience to consider an alternative narrative and a new story to live out.

Performers are driven by a compelling vision and are fuelled by the desire to translate that vision into something meaningful for their audience. Most artists know that they will only achieve an extraordinary performance if they constantly push themselves to evolve and upgrade.

They will be diligent and rigorous in their practice and rehearsal. They will hone and refine the necessary skills and behaviours. Feedback will be expected from the start of any project and the artist will actively seek it out, as they know that it only serves to enhance the end product.

Sitting right at the very heart of all this is an attitude, a mindset and a way of thinking that binds everything together. It is *this* that creates *extraordinary.* Having the right behaviours and skills in isolation is not enough. At the core of any artist's own development, it will be their attitude and mindset that take centre stage, as without this pointing in the right direction, everything else falls away and the results are plain old beige!

In the same way, organizations have a performance to put on 24/7. They have an audience to engage with. People that they need to reach out to and connect with. A story to tell. Hearts and minds to win over. A purpose. A quality service to deliver. An experience to create that the audience will want to return to again and again. A brand to maintain. Stakeholders that want to be listened to and heard. A culture that goes viral for all the *right* reasons. A culture that their own performers will want to be a part of and can thrive in. A place where people are rewarded for what they deliver and how they deliver it. An organization that every stakeholder believes is extraordinary.

I can safely say that every performer and leader I have come across in the last 20 years, who is striving for extraordinary, has bravely chosen the attitudes, behaviours and thinking patterns that need to be left behind while holding on to those that will propel them forward. Without a Jolt, it can be easy and comfortable to keep churning out more of the same. Ultimately though, in some guise, the Jolt will appear!

I remember it well ...

I have had many Jolts in my lifetime. Some I noticed, some I probably didn't. Some I reacted well to, some I rolled on the floor, kicked my feet in the air and screamed like a baby (age 33 was the last one of those and it wasn't pretty!). The Jolts that stand out, many of which I wrestled with, have become my guiding principles and are now a part of how I navigate my day. Experience has shown me that they are the basis for building anything extraordinary.

> Jolt is not a thing that you do. Jolt is not your outcome. Jolt is a way of being.

In 1995 I joined the West End cast of The Phantom of the Opera. The Phantom company and the many gorgeous people within it became my home, on and off, for many years. My time there was a rich tapestry of learning about the craft of consistently creating something extraordinary. On numerous occasions I was left baffled over why we would yet again spend hours practising tiny pieces of music and staging. Surely something so small couldn't make a difference to the show? How would an audience ever notice? It was already a worldwide phenomenon, grossing millions globally through ticket sales and merchandise. Why fiddle with it?

Wind the clock forward 18 years and my wisdom and learning is in a more rounded place to make sense of it all. Delivering something extraordinary, eight times a week, is a feat even for the most experienced and seasoned performers and musicians. The courage and hunger to continually reinvent takes energy and tenacity. If we let go of that, we switch onto auto-pilot, turn off the radar and deliver a lacklustre performance. In the world of the arts, there is no place for that.

So why is it then that in the world of business we often accept that as being ok?

A while into my run at Phantom, the resident director took me to one side and offered me a dollop of wisdom. I am grateful that he did as I believe it dramatically changed the course of my existence and placed the importance of Jolt right at the heart of what I do. He brought it to my attention that I had entered a 'safe zone' – a place that delivered an ordinary performance and not an extraordinary one. I had become comfortable and was delivering just enough each night.

The feedback and challenge he offered me was very clear.

> 'Richard, what you do on stage each night is ok. It's fine. It won't change the world though. However, I'm not sure that deep down you are happy with ok and fine, are you?'

> 'Not entirely, no. BUT what if I step it up a gear and then screw it up? What if I test out new ways and they fail? What if it doesn't work? What if I crack a note? That all feels like a big risk to take!'

He smiled at me yet delivered a message that walloped me between the eyes!

> 'The greatest risk Richard is not that you step it up a gear and do something differently. The risk is not that you give it a go and fail either. The greatest risk is that you stay doing the same thing, day in and day out, eight times a week. If you do, you won't have a job and we won't have a show. I'm telling you now so that you can make your best choice.'

The Jolt that came from my director shook me up. It was a very clear choice point for me. Doing nothing would cost me big time. Looking back on that moment, I smile to myself as I realize how naive I had been to believe that there was no risk to me in staying doing the same thing, over and over again.

Jolts will come in all shapes and sizes. They may well wallop your arse when you least expect it. They may knock you to your knees. Hear this though, what makes the difference between an enabling Jolt and a disabling Jolt is how YOU choose to respond to it. Jolts will be sudden, uncomfortable, provocative and create a heightened state of awareness of your thinking, your action and the situation you are in.

> Will you embrace the Jolts around you or will you fight them off?

Time to make an upgrade

Imagine using technology that is 20 years out of date – analogue TV, cassettes, Atari computers. Even operating on a Windows system that is three years old can cause problems. It will work up to a point and yet when you need to engage and connect with your audience, it may well let you down. Technology upgrades have become normal in our world. What you buy today will have a new version available tomorrow. As I sit waiting for my iPhone 6 to arrive, I do so in the knowledge that even by tomorrow, new software upgrades will have been made available. If you are truly committed to making the step from ordinary to extraordinary, the starting point is to decide what upgrades are necessary. You may well have some catching up to do if you haven't upgraded for many years!

When did you last make an upgrade to *your* current version?

Upgrading will quickly become a regular habit *if* you choose to make it so. When you have your radar switched on and are truly in the moment, you will start to notice the choices you make that are working and those that let you down.

Choices is an important word in the last sentence and will feature a great deal in this book. Look out for it. I will offer you plenty of choice points in each Jolt. This will be your opportunity to decide. A moment in time when you can choose to stay operating on the old version, or you can dare yourself to do something different and make the upgrade. The more choices you have available, the more flexible you can be.

> Those with the greatest flexibility will have the greatest influence.

In this book, I will present you with a series of upgrades; bite-size nuggets that will disrupt your thinking and call you to action. Something that will shake you up. Give you a Jolt! This is a book that you can dip in and dip out of. Leave it on your desk. Swat flies with it. Chuck it across the room in frustration. Read it. Learn from it. Share it around. Take it to the loo with you. Steal quotes from it and send them to your friends. Whatever you do, use the messages contained within to help you, and those around you, to dance at the edge of extraordinary.

For ease, I have broken the book into two distinct parts, Part 1 and Part 2.

Part 1 is going to lay out some building blocks. I am going to give you a framework for you to hang all your future learning from. I am going to show you how often you place your attention and focus on the *wrong* things and then wonder why you didn't get what you had hoped for. When I first learnt this stuff, it blew my mind in one almighty Jolt. Part 1 will give you the understanding you need in order to move through the Jolts. I am sure you are eager to get deep into the Jolts but please take the time to thoroughly read this part first.

Part 2 is where you will find the Jolts hanging out. These are the nuggets that you can use to move yourself from ordinary to extraordinary. Each one will contain a call to action, an *Artful* illustration of why this upgrade matters and then the point where I hand *Over to You*; your opportunity to stop, think and choose your next move, before committing to take action.

Some Jolts will be short and sharp whilst others will pull your thinking in various directions and will require greater time to reflect. I will weave stories throughout that demonstrate the power of the Jolt. You will find some photos of me naked. Some photos of you naked (don't ask how I got them …) Mostly there will be bucket loads of learning and insight.

Your call to action!

Let's be honest, what we are playing with here at the most basic level is habit change: getting rid of the habits that no longer work and installing some new and more up-to-date ones. The key thing with habit change is that it requires the initial insight for you to see that you may just need to do something differently:

How do you know if what you are doing works well or not?

When did you last ask your audience for their perspective?

When were you last present enough to notice if you still had them seduced?

From this point, habit change requires a desire to upgrade, a dose of persistence, some consistency and a shove from the norm. That's exactly what you'll get here. As your own personal coach, I will ask you the questions that get you thinking – then I need to hand over to you as it is YOU that ultimately makes the choice to remain ordinary or not …

You may want to jot things down as you go along. Capture everything that resonates with you along the way. Sometimes writing it down in your own language will help you lock it in. You can just scribble your ideas next to mine. A well-thumbed book will be your evidence that the messages are landing!

Whatever the many things are that you ultimately decide to do with the contents of this book, do one thing:

Take action!

Read a piece. Digest what it means for you. Dare yourself to tackle it. Look in the mirror and commit to how you will test out the ideas. Act. Then notice what bounces back.

> Motion creates Emotion. By getting up and doing, acting it out, walking differently, talking differently, you will begin to alter your thinking, attitude, mood and emotion. Don't take my word for it. Take your word for it!

It's important at this stage to remind you that the one and only thing you are in absolute control of is your thinking, your responses, your feelings and your behaviour. I will keep reminding you of that throughout the book, just in case it slips your mind. Too often you may forget this and attempt to control outcomes that are not actually yours to control.

> The one and only thing you are in absolute control of is your thinking, your responses, your feelings and your behaviour.

I want you to have fun with this stuff. Life can be serious at times and requires you to deal with it seriously. That doesn't mean that you need to take yourself so seriously! Get playful. Laugh and indulge in your successes and laugh at your foibles and mistakes – there will be many. This stuff is simple. It doesn't come with guarantees. It's not easy either. After all, if it were easy and guaranteed, you would have already done it by now, wouldn't you? To take on the Jolts and adopt an Artful approach as a part of your daily practice will certainly get you closer to extraordinary. It will also stretch you to work at your very edge …

The same is true for you right now as it was for me in my Phantom days. The greatest risk is not that you embrace the ideas from this book, test them out and dare yourself to fail. No, the greatest risk is that you continue doing the same things that have got you to this point, over and over again, in the hope that they will bring you even greater success.

So, clench your buttock cheeks, breathe deep and let the extraordinary performance unfold.

Richard Tyler
Chief Possibility Architect
2015

Part 1
Setting the Scene

'Noticing is the art of all arts.'

Henry David Thoreau

Who do you see in the mirror?

Deeply etched in my memory is the very first time I ever stood in front of a totally mirrored wall at Music College. Dance classes were a required part of the curriculum for everyone, regardless of what course you were on. The idea behind it was that dance taught core strength, discipline and the ability to use your body well (whatever that means …).

Now, anyone who knows me will be well aware that any style of dancing is not really my thing. My body was just not made for dancing. Someone once asked me in a nightclub if I was having a fit – I was just enjoying the music and bopping around in my own way!

Anyway, there I stood in my black leotard and jazz shoes, gazing at myself in the floor to ceiling mirror. I was fairly shocked. How can one person look a complete idiot in such a simple outfit? I thought it must be the mirrors that offered the warped view but quickly realized that it was, in fact, me. It was excruciatingly uncomfortable. I didn't like the instant feedback that I was getting. I felt incredibly vulnerable and even if I averted my gaze, I was still only aware of the 6ft dancing ironing board I could see in front of me.

I will talk much more about the feedback loop that exists within the performance arena later on. Performers rely heavily on that constant choice point that comes with feedback. The belief is that each insight offers the opportunity to make an upgrade, to hit refresh and to Jolt.

When did you last proactively seek out feedback and insight from your team and your audience?

So, before we go any further into the book, I want **you** to take a look in the mirror. Don't worry; you don't need to wear a leotard for this, unless you really want to! You can go and look in a real mirror if it helps, otherwise the mirror in your own mind will work just as well.

★ Over to You

Not everyone I invite to do this is up for it. Looking in the mirror can be uncomfortable. If you're serious about making an upgrade and smooching with extraordinary, this reflection time is critical.

With every choice you make, comes a consequence. Choosing to look at yourself comes with a consequence, as does deciding to skip this part …

…You choose.

If you are genuinely determined to dance with extraordinary, looking in the mirror will need to become a part of your core practice. Self-reflection presents you with the opportunity to transform.

As you now begin to gaze through the Artful lens, it is time to share with you the core principles that are the essence of an extraordinary performance. When you begin to hone each one, you too will edge closer towards extraordinary …

Now consider the following questions. Take enough time to do this well. Scribble down your answers.

Daring: How much time do you currently spend 'daring' yourself? These are the moments when your inner chatter encourages you to push beyond, have a go, create a rumpus, dream big and push harder. These are the moments when you *hear* your *enabling* inner chatter and act on it. How much do you currently dare others? When do you cajole your team into flirting with extraordinary or when do you leave them being ordinary?

Connection: How well do you connect with your audience? When did you last check in with them to understand if they are getting what they need? How have you upgraded the way in which you connect? When did you last ask them what they need from you to be delivering an extraordinary experience?

Impact: How well do you make an impact? We all know folks that can make an impact in a negative way by being mood hoovers, dismissive, rude, unaware … but where does your brand truly land well with your audience? Where does it let you down? Where are you turning your audience off?

Possibility: How much time do you spend carving out what is possible as opposed to what is *impossible*? How would your colleagues describe your use of questions and teasing out of new thinking? How well do you shift negative thoughts, your own and those of others, into possibility?

Radar on: Having your radar on means being present – in that moment only with your peripheral vision and awareness ramped up to full. **Only** in this state will you create choices. How much of your day do you spend with the radar on and up? In what situations? With whom? When are you so lost in your own thoughts that you fail to even switch the radar on?

Invention: When you trip yourself up and get in your own way, how well do you invent new thinking and new actions that will allow you to move forward? How much of the *new story* for your organization are you inventing, dreaming and sharing? Where do you dream small and where do you dream BIG?

Feedback loop: Are you a part of a feedback culture? How do you role model the receiving and giving of high quality insights? When did you last offer real precision *feedforward*? When did you last review your own input? When did you last actively seek out feedback from your audience?

Commitment: How would you describe your commitment to achieving the extraordinary? In what contexts are you driven to keep exploring all opportunities and pushing each one to its edge? Where are you in 'try' mode – that state where there is no sense of failing and yet no hunger to be the best version of yourself either? On a scale of 0–10 (10 REALLY wanting extraordinary outcomes), where would you say you spend most of your day?

Vulnerability: Howard Shultz, CEO of Starbucks, once said that: 'The hardest part about being a leader is demonstrating or showing vulnerability.' How comfortable are you with leaving your ego at the door? It is easy to get drawn into a cycle of needing to be seen as a strong action hero. Do you view your own vulnerability as a strength? Where are you comfortable displaying vulnerability and where are you not?

Lots of questions to ponder, so it is worth spending a little extra time on this part. Some of the questions will have provoked a sharp intake of breath, others less so. However, the ones that hit a nerve are the ones to tinker with first.

Now, with each of those principles I want you to consider your Upgrade; what is your new version for each of the above? If you were truly committed to bringing your hardware and software up to date to deliver extraordinary outcomes for your audience, what would you now need to do differently?

Write it down. Make it specific. Make sure it is something that will add significant value. Consider how it will make a difference to your audience.

We will tease these upgrades out in more detail as you work through the book, but for now, if you were to announce each upgrade, what would you tell people? Again, write it down. Seeing it in front of you, in your own handwriting, changes the way you respond to it, which ultimately impacts the action that you will take. Part of your quest towards becoming extraordinary will be that you announce your outcomes and upgrades. I often observe leaders who leave their outcomes and upgrades sitting quietly in a corner of their heads, deep in the belief that if they don't tell people then no one will hold them to account. The trouble with that is that the very act of someone holding you to account, and you holding yourself accountable, sits at the core of being extraordinary. It demonstrates your commitment, how daring you are, and will be the cue for those around you to do the same.

> Announce your upgrades and then be accountable for what you do and do not deliver!

Playing at your edge

'Oooh no, I couldn't possibly do that. It's way out of my comfort zone ...'

I frequently hear that phrase trotted out by people. It rolls off the tongue with such ease and is habitually used as a justification for why they can't do something or don't want to dare themselves enough. Maybe you've also used it before? Like most things in life, if you tell yourself something over and over again it soon becomes the truth in your head and therefore your reality. This will be the same for the enabling stories you tell yourself as the disabling ones!

When I hear the statement above, I usually follow up with a few questions:

How do you know that your comfort zone is *there*?

Were you born with it right *there*?

Can you not move it?!

The truth of the matter is: comfort zones are a pure invention. There, I said it.

Take some time and ask yourself the following questions. Again, it's a good idea to scribble down your answers. If you are eager to get on to the Jolts, you could easily skip this bit. Stay with it. Give this some time now. The more personal insight you gain now, the quicker you will be able to play with the Jolts.

Where does your own comfort zone come out to play?

In what situations do you tell yourself, or others, that what is being asked of you is out of your comfort zone?

Can you see your comfort zone? Touch it? Does it feel different when you knock against it?

In what way does it help you or hinder you?

What would it take for you to move it or blow it up?

Don't get me wrong; when you first invented your 'comfort zone' and decided where to put it, it would have been the right choice for you in that precise moment. As we have already agreed though, the world has moved on. Your 'comfort zone' was a fabulous invention for keeping you safe. The question to ask yourself right now though is this:

> If you were to leave your comfort zone exactly where it is, how will it help you achieve what you want?

Will it help you?

Will it be a lever towards extraordinary?

In many of the workshops I run, we bring in a handful of the most extraordinary musicians. Together we unwrap the components of music, singing and performance as an immersive experience, for leaders to learn what being extraordinary really means. Rather than just building the intellectual understanding, which most people get easily, deep learning and change come about when people are in it, doing it and being it. I'm well aware that working in this way presses plenty of hot buttons, provokes discomfort and yet also unlocks immense possibility. When I spot a hot button, chances are I want to press it. You have been warned.

I recently ran a workshop where a particularly senior leader from the organization was resisting the chance to sing on his own in front of his colleagues. (I can sense you are already eager to be a part of one of my workshops …).

His reasoning? *'It's out of my comfort zone!'*

What ensued was a bizarre scene that some might believe was set up in advance to illustrate a point. If only I were clever enough to set something like this up.

'So, tell me what's going on?'

'It's way too far out of my comfort zone to sing on my own…'

'Ok, show me whereabouts your comfort zone is …'

He marked out the boundary with absolute precision …

'It starts about … here.'

'Ok, if I were to pick it up and say ... move it over here, would you then be more comfortable to sing?'

'Oh yes, sure I would.'

'Ok, let's do that then ...'

I moved his comfort zone (not really ... as it wasn't actually there!), he stood up and proceeded to sing to the group. When he finished, he looked at me expectantly.

'My mother always told me to put things back exactly where I found them so let me just move it back to ... here ... that's where it was wasn't it?'

'Yep, that's about it.'

'So, would you now get up and sing again?'

'Ha. You're joking. No way!'

Aren't people fabulous? It was the most bizarre scenario played out by someone who genuinely believed this thing existed. Simply by moving his *invented comfort zone*, something that had not been possible suddenly became possible.

I went on to explain to him that his comfort zone was not really a thing that I could move. It isn't an actual wall that physically stops you in your tracks. You don't really brush up against it. Yet sometimes that is exactly how it feels.

I am amazed at the number of times I observe very bright and switched on leaders shy away from the buttock-clenching opportunities that sit in front of them. They hit a choice point that most of them don't even notice as they are running on auto-pilot. The habit kicks in, they tell themselves it is out of their 'comfort zone' and they close down the opportunity.

There is a common theme in every instance – the comfort zone is a myth! The moment they sail close to anything that feels as if it could be their edge, their limit or their boundary, they know that by pushing a notch further, they will begin to open up the possibility of creating something different and therefore the potential to be extraordinary. The hunger for extraordinary is so strong there is rarely any negotiation required.

At some point, once you have practised this enough, it will become your new habit. Until that time arrives, I have a few questions to help get you moving. Take a moment to think about a situation you currently have on your radar where you know you are stuck with your 'comfort zone' limitation … Got one? Good …

What does having your comfort zone right there do for you?

In what way does it protect you and serve you well?

What is the risk in doing that?

What is the opportunity?

You may not feel comfortable enough to put dynamite sticks under your 'comfort zone' yet, of course. So if you were to move it by just a notch, perhaps even something as small as 1 degree, what would that allow you to do differently now?

★ Over to You

Taking these Jolts, making an upgrade and heading for extraordinary will undoubtedly require you to *move* or explode your invented 'comfort zone'.

So, are you going to leave it where it is or budge it somewhere else? Every choice comes with consequences ...

It might be as simple as in my story – you pick it up and move it without any fuss.

If it doesn't feel quite that easy yet, revisit the questions above and now decide on your next move.

The path to extraordinary ... one small step at a time

In the introduction to this book, I explained how skills and behaviours in isolation are not enough to reach extraordinary. Yet, still, an exorbitant amount of money and energy is spent by organizations every year developing them as standalone pieces. In my experience, this is a big mistake. The American Society for Training and Development (ASTD) reports that for 2012 alone, US organizations spent an eye-watering $164.2 billion (yes, BILLION) on training staff. I can't claim to have seen every development programme on the planet, yet I know from my own clients that much of the training they deliver, historically, consists of developing skills and behaviours only. While this is of course important, it is not enough if organizations truly want to embrace a new story, a new way of thinking with an attitude that crafts more *extraordinary* moments than just *ordinary* ones.

Over the next few pages, I am going to explain the reasons for why I see it this way.

Think for a moment about what it is that right now stands between you and extraordinary.

A lack of time, a lack of ambition, too much *other stuff to do*, lack of courage or perhaps an absence of natural talent? Sadly, many of the people that I have coached over the years believe it is the latter. Really? How much do you believe that a lack of natural talent truly limits what you are capable of?

Well, in 95% of cases, it doesn't!

Benjamin Bloom, an eminent educational researcher, studied 120 outstanding achievers. They were made up of concert pianists, sculptors, Olympic swimmers, world-class tennis players, mathematicians and research neurologists. Most had not been that remarkable as children and didn't show signs of clear talent before their training began in earnest. Bloom concluded: 'After 40 years of intensive research on school learning in the United States as well as abroad, my major conclusion is this: What any person in the world can learn, almost all persons can learn, if provided with the appropriate prior and current conditions of learning.' He's not including the 2 to 3% of children who have severe impairments, and he's not counting the top 1 to 2% of children at the other extreme … He is, though, counting everybody else.

Ok, I want to ruffle up your thinking a bit. I want to show you something now that will change the way you make choices and decisions forever. I can't brainwash you into absorbing this thinking – only you can do that by taking these ideas and pushing them around your own mind for a while, which in turn will ignite new action.

Imagine this: you are now sitting in a large room full of around 100 people. Some of them you know and some of them you don't. I am standing at the front and ready to guide you through some learning. During this session I am going to influence you to do something. I want to push you to your edge to see what it takes for you to step over. Some in the room will tumble easily, others less so.

The challenge: I am going to teach you a short song that the entire group will sing. Easy. We will all give some immediate feedback, think about how we can upgrade it and we will then run it through once more. Still fairly easy.

Now, after that part, I want you to come up to the front of the room and sing the same song, only this time, on your own …

At this stage, what happens in your mind? What does your inner chatter start to say to yourself – 'I can't sing, I hate singing, I'll look stupid, he's joking, WOW what an opportunity, I love to sing, I'm here to learn so I'll give it a twirl ...'. Take a moment to think about what your response and your reaction to the idea of singing solo is.

It's ok, relax. I'm going to help you. Let's think about what it would take to make this happen for you. I will talk you through my Performance Map step by step. Off we go ...

1. SPACE: I understand that singing in this environment may be extremely uncomfortable for you and will see you bashing your 'invented' comfort zone. However, do you find yourself singing in the rain (see what I did there?!), bath, kitchen, car, karaoke? Are you a shower singer?

I appreciate that singing in *this* space though, with *these* people could well be uncomfortable, so how about we change the space you are in? What if you were to be in a room, just you, away from these people and you can sing the same song but this time on your own?

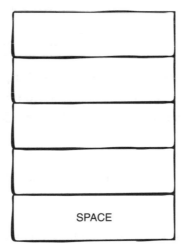

Would that make it more comfortable for you? Would you now sing having made a tiny adaptation to the space you are in?

Ok, here's the next change we can make ...

2. ACTION: I will give you a 10 minute 1:1 coaching session on the ACTION of an extraordinary singer. ACTION is the 'behaviour of' ... in this instance, the behaviours of an extraordinary singer. So during that 10-minute session I will help you learn how a singer moves, gets themselves on the stage, what they do to engage their audience and how they get themselves off stage at the end. It will be quite straightforward and you will soon have the required actions to 'do' singing.

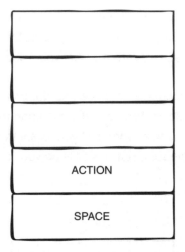

Are you in now or not? Having learnt the ACTION, would you be more comfortable getting up and giving it a go in front of this group? So we will keep the SPACE the same and you will have learnt the ACTION that you need. Deal?

You may be bought in already and you may not. I'll add to the deal to make easier for you ...

3. SKILLS: I will give you a 20-minute 1:1 coaching session on the SKILLS of an extraordinary singer. This is the 'how to' part and will cover basic technique: producing a note, pitching a note and diaphragmatic breathing. This will mean that after 20 minutes of focused learning, you will have the ACTION (what a singer does) and the SKILLS (how a singer does it). By default, this will begin to change your thinking. Having those two pieces in place will start to nudge your own belief away from something that disables you, towards something that is more enabling and begins to open up possibility.

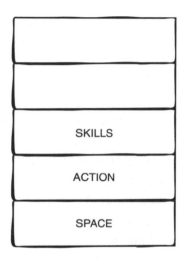

Does this now do it for you? Would you feel more comfortable getting up and giving it a go? Think about it for moment ... You may not love it, that's for sure. The outcome is not to love it though. The outcome is to give it a go and see what's possible. Are you on for doing it now? Sure?

Let's change the game a bit. Up to now we have made some fairly straightforward adaptations in order to get a different outcome:

- change the SPACE (where you do it),
- upgrade your ACTION (what you do) and
- develop your SKILLS (how you do it).

All of these elements we can see around us and can be easy to tinker with. If you don't like something, you can change the SPACE and go somewhere else. By changing your ACTION, you can affect the outcome. Learning new SKILLS will help give you more choices for 'how' you do something.

Now let's move this on another step …

4. THINK: I now want to share something with you that will present you with far greater choice if you begin to fiddle around with it. I will work with you 1:1 for 30 minutes to help you decide how you could THINK differently about what is being asked of you in order that your ACTION upgrades.

THINK is made up of two elements: values and beliefs.

Values are your highest held criteria in life: the things that matter most to you and the principles that you live by. It is rare for any of us to navigate our day consciously thinking about our values and beliefs, they sit there though, ticking away, driving the choices we make and the ACTION we take. Some of my values are trust, integrity, fun, difference, honesty, commitment, curiosity … it would be a long list if I shared them all with you.

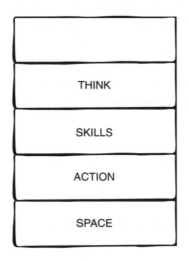

THINK

SKILLS

ACTION

SPACE

What are your values? What is most important to you? Take a moment now to write them down. Some will immediately fall out of your head, others will require more thought.

Generally in life, our paths will cross with many people that we share common values with. This happens in organizations a great deal. Values may be freely discussed and many people will express their agreement and understanding. Some organizations even choose to emblazon their corridors and meeting rooms with their values as a reminder to all stakeholders of what matters most. Problems can arise though when people think they are talking about the same thing – 'Ah yes, trust is important to me too …' – but unless we take the time to truly understand what trust means to the other person, this is meaningless. Your evidence and criteria for trust might well be very different to mine. If we fail to share this, then we are likely to hit some kind of disagreement. It frequently comes out to play at performance review time and appraisals. The manager and their reports will sit down and agree some areas to develop. Words will be used that both parties nod at in total agreement and understanding: more trust, bigger risks, greater honesty. They remain hollow words unless one person is sharp enough to ask some more probing questions:

What does having more trust mean to you?

How would you know that I trust you?

What would be the three things that you would see me doing that would symbolize greater trust?

What can we agree to do if we don't see those behaviours?

In thinking about your own values that you listed above, what do you need to do at an ACTION level that would demonstrate you living out each value?

Values are learnt. They will have been modelled for you by your family, friends, culture, schooling, workplace etc. You may have practised and rehearsed them over time, so will have little day-to-day conscious awareness of this. Of course, your values can also change throughout life as your circumstances change. When my daughter was born, my values hierarchy shifted around no end. Some things that had once been important became less so and others moved up the list to take pride of place at the top.

Your values will guide your daily choices and ACTION.

The second element of THINK is beliefs.

Beliefs are your inner script: your rights, wrongs, shoulds, should nots, dos, do nots, musts, must nots. Over time they become your rules. I tend to break them down into two distinct types of belief: those that are *enabling* beliefs and those that are *disabling*. With practice and rehearsal, whether they are disabling or enabling they will eventually become your habit. You will rarely think about them as they just continue quietly functioning in the background.

Standing at the airport last year, I was witness to a short scenario played out by a young family. The girl was about 3 and clearly very excited at the sight of a giant aeroplane landing in front of her very eyes. Her excitement was alive and she shared it with those around her through a series of high-pitched screeching sessions. Admittedly this was at a frequency that attracted small dogs, yet I could appreciate that a 3-year-old needed to express her wonder and amazement in some way! Her parents had probably seen hundreds of planes in their time and were not sharing in her wonder. The dad turned to his daughter and said, '*I have told you before, children are there to be seen and not heard. Now zip it.*'

Jolt!!! Hers, not mine. The only thing was that at the age of 3 she was unlikely to find or take any useful learning from it. I was completely dumbfounded and yet recognized that it was none of my business. I was shocked though that people still carried that belief around and passed it onto others. How many times had the dad heard that as a child, which meant he now needed to share it with his own daughter? Consequently, on how many occasions will she need to hear it before it becomes her truth and her belief too?

As a coach, I work with lots of leaders who want to find their own voice: speak up, make a contribution, share ideas, challenge, be heard and get noticed. It is very rare indeed to find someone that has a physiological vocal issue that stops them from finding and using their voice. Most people are born with the most awesome instrument to use. At some point in their lives though, they will have had an experience that resulted in them closing down their true voice and, as we have discussed already, if this is practised enough then it can quickly become the new habit. I work on the basis that most of the issues I am asked to help tackle are not 'born in' problems. They have been learnt. And as we know, anything that has been learnt can also be unlearnt.

> From within the depths of your mind, your own THINKING (your values and beliefs) will be guiding your daily ACTIONS.

Back to the singing for a moment. What was your inner chatter at the time of being asked to sing in front of this group? What beliefs enabled you and which ones disabled you?

Whenever I ask this question, I tend to get the following responses from those that **wanted** to get up and give it a go:

Why not, I'm here to learn and stretch myself...?

I know I can't sing and most of the people will be no better or worse than me so I gave it a go!

So what if it's rubbish? I like singing. The group may laugh at me or with me. It doesn't change anything.

I live by the belief of I'll give it a whirl ...

I thought I had to do it so decided to get it done first.

I figured that you and the team would give me some feedback on how to improve. You can only do that if I get up and have a go.

Those are all beliefs that *enabled* an individual to test it out, open the possibility and have a go.

And from those folks that resisted:

I can't sing so what's the point?

I'd look stupid. I'm not a singer!

I know I can't sing as my family tell me so all the time.

I would have been up for it after five pints ...

You'd have to have paid me ...

I didn't get up because I didn't believe that doing this would add any value to my life whatsoever!

How fascinating! Which group would your response have fallen into? Enabling or disabling?

> Change your THINKING and you open up the possibility to change your ACTION!

The last response was interesting and prompted an open group dialogue with the person that shared it. She was a very senior leader from a global financial institution. The sharpness in her response was very evident – not just to me but to the other 50 people in the room.

'I didn't get up because I didn't believe that doing this would add any value to my life whatsoever!'

'Can I just ask you then, when did you last get up and sing, on your own, in front of this group?'

'Well, I haven't … ever!'

*'So, how do you know that getting up now and singing, in front of this group, wouldn't add the **greatest** value to your life EVER? How do you truly know that …?'*

'… I don't!'

JOLT!!

The point I intended to make, landed. It was a Jolt that she was not expecting. And it landed with the rest of the room too. Your beliefs are practised and become wonderful inventions on all those occasions when they help you get the outcome you want. You will live by them as you think, on the whole, that they serve you well. That belief did in fact work for the lady, in as much as it meant she *didn't* have to sing at that moment. There was another question to consider though, that she hadn't asked: *'How do I really know that doing this (singing in this example …) won't add massive value to my life if there is no previous experience to base it on?'*

Despite the belief she held giving her some protection and safety in that moment, it didn't allow for any new possibilities to be explored. Just imagine that there was an opportunity to be seized by coming to the front of the room and singing: an opportunity that could have changed her life in some way, forever. She wouldn't have discovered it though, as her habitual belief kept running on autopilot. She hadn't taken the slightest pause to consider an alternative way of thinking that might perhaps bring about an alternative outcome.

After coffee break that morning, the lady came to me and asked me if there was an opportunity to speak with the group. *'Yes, sure there is'*, I replied. When everyone was back in the room, the lady came to the front, thanked me for my challenge and shared with the group what she had just experienced. Despite the discomfort of me challenging her, she had recognized that her thinking was generally so rapid that she hardly ever made space to consider what her outcome was or to find a new way to get it. From someone who had been so abrupt and dismissive she was now displaying great vulnerability. Before we knew it she was singing a short nursery rhyme to the group. Massive applause followed. Had we just discovered the next Beyonce? No. With some work, who knows, but it wasn't about the singing. What we discovered was far more important and relevant – pushing at the edges of your THINKING opens up possibility. And opening up possibility sits at the heart of creating something extraordinary.

> Being extraordinary requires you to first seek out all possibilities.

I recognize that you might now be muttering in your head that you don't want to be a singer and you did not buy into a book about singing. Correct. This is not about singing. The book is not about turning you into a singer. This book is about jolting you to be an extraordinary leader as opposed to an ordinary one. I don't mind what beliefs you hold about your own ability to sing. I DO, however, care about the beliefs you hold and the THINKING that you do that stops you from being an extraordinary leader. I DO care what you THINK, and therefore believe, about your relationships, feedback, power, risk, influence, accountability, delegation, bravery, impact, presenting yourself and communication as this will all determine how much of an extraordinary leader you become.

Exploring possibilities in life requires you to choose the most suitable THINKING, which in turn will allow you to notice the choices that are in front of you. Without that upgrade to your THINKING, the possibilities will remain limited.

> When you start to upgrade your THINKING and refresh your ACTION, your outcomes will shift.

When Stephen R. Covey first created habit 4 of the 7 in his book *The 7 Habits of Highly Effective People*, it was called Win-Win. He then added a simple word that made all the difference: *THINK* Win-Win. This was the cue for the reader to elevate it from an ACTION and SKILL to THINKING. Covey knew that simply *doing* Win-Win would not be enough or sustainable without the appropriate THINKING and attitude to support it.

Back to my challenge to you then: if you were to invent a new piece of enabling THINKING that would make it possible for you to sing as opposed to resisting it, what would that need to be? It's just an invention and doesn't need to be the 'right one'. It only needs to invite you to test this out. After you've got up and done it, you can either store it as a new upgrade, or delete it.

So, are you now in, or out? To sing a solo or not sing a solo, that is the question …?

By this point, you will have probably found a way to get yourself up and singing. Of course you may still be fighting with yourself over this. And possibly with me!

There's one more piece to fiddle with …

5. IDENTITY: I am a singer. It is a part of who I am, through and through. I choose not to do the ACTION of singing anymore, as it's no longer what gives me my thrills in life. At an IDENTITY level though, it is still very much a part of who I am. Music, singing, performance are all a massive part of what I stand for.

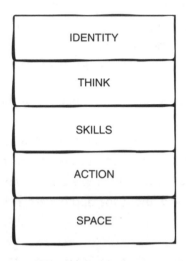

I have multiple identities operating. It's ok, it's not something I need therapy for. I am a parent, a son, a brother, a friend, a coach, a speaker …

All of those are far more than just ACTIONS for me. They are not simply something that I do, they are fundamental to who I am and what I think I am here for.

However, there are plenty of things I can do that are NOT a part of my IDENTITY.

I can cook: providing I am in my SPACE (my kitchen), I have all the right ACTIONS (know what to do in the kitchen to prepare a meal), thanks to my Ottolenghi cookbook I have the SKILLS (recipe and the steps needed to make it) and I have the right THINKING (I don't believe anyone will die from eating my food – well, they haven't yet!). However, at IDENTITY level, I am NOT a chef. It is something I can do and not something that I am.

The difference? When I hold something at IDENTITY level, I commit to it very differently from when it is just an ACTION that I do. I take far more accountability for the outcome.

Let me ask you a question, are you a leader or do you do the ACTION of leadership? Are you a manager or do you do the ACTION of management? These are extremely different things. If you just DO leadership and management, without the connection at an IDENTITY level, your audience becomes DONE to. In all my work with leaders over the years, the ones that stand out at delivering extraordinary outcomes are those that connect with their role at an identity level. They have taken it on as a part of who they are. The ones I have seen struggling to engage, connect and generally make sustainable stuff happen, are those that DO the ACTION alone of leadership. They treat it as a task to tick off the list. Their teams and stakeholders then become a task to be done. Who wants to be a task that is done?! Not me! Do you?!

Imagine for a second that when you get up to sing, you take on the IDENTITY of a singer – now have a big resounding, *I am a singer!* ringing in your head. Go on, say it to yourself. This alone, of course, will not be enough. You will need to couple it with your new THINKING (enabling belief) and the SKILLS and the ACTION that you have learnt from our 1:1 sessions.

Perhaps you are still hankering after your five pints in order to do this … but where do you think five pints sits within this model? Yes! It sits at THINK level. When you are in a karaoke bar and have had copious buckets of booze, I am sorry to break the news that your SKILL does not change. You cannot suddenly sing any better than you could 5 minutes before. What changes is your THINKING:

I am Beyonce! I can sing like Pavarotti! Everyone wants to listen to me! I am the greatest! Who cares if I'm rubbish, it's not about being the best …

Your THINKING upgrades thanks to the alcohol, but sadly your SKILL doesn't! The change in THINKING gives the illusion of confidence. That illusion enables you to give it your best shot and commit to it with little concern about the fallout.

I am an advocate of leadership without alcohol! Your THINKING needs to upgrade as and when required. No beer needed.

We have based our Performance Map on the work of Robert Dilts and the Neurological Levels model that he developed from some earlier work by Gregory Bateson. It offers a way for you to check where your focus and attention needs to be in order that you get the best outcomes. This model will be central to all action you take from the Jolts in this book and on your quest towards becoming extraordinary.

Consider this: all of us will operate out of every level at any one time.

> You are always within a SPACE (the pub, your office, a boardroom, toilet cubicle …).

> You are always demonstrating some kind of ACTION (this is the behaviour that you are doing whilst in that SPACE).

> This is backed up by SKILL (how you do that ACTION).

> This is driven by your THINKING (your values and beliefs that both enable and disable).

> This is ultimately driven by IDENTITY (who you are and what you stand for).

> Making a change to any level will affect your outcome.

Take this scenario. Fred has a relationship that he is keen to improve. Much rests on the success of this collaboration in delivering a new project for his audience. However, Fred doesn't rate Jane much. In fact, he thinks she's pretty useless. She has let him down a few times with lack of delivery and poor quality work. He now believes she doesn't add value. Every meeting they have seems to be fractious and they both leave with little being achieved.

There are a few options:

Change the SPACE – meet somewhere else, get off-site, go to a new location in order to Jolt the previous experiences.

Fred could just take new ACTION – behaving in a way that shows he respects her, likes her and wants her to succeed. He could turn up the charm, listen more, change his tone of voice and adapt his body language; there are many behavioural shifts that could make a difference.

Learn some new SKILLS – maybe Fred doesn't know *how* to build a good relationship and needs to go on a course to help him learn.

Fred could shift his THINKING – positive behaviours at an ACTION level, with out-of-date THINKING, are unlikely to move this forward. Jane will experience incongruence and a mixed message. As the THINKING part ('she's useless, lets me down, doesn't add any value …') has been practised for far longer so will be dominant to any new ACTION.

Make an IDENTITY tweak – I AM flexible and adaptable and I am a leader that can make this relationship work.

Dilts' key learning point from this model is crucial. I'm going to say it a few times as I need you to hear it loud and clear! The higher the level you make some change and adaptation, the more sustainable your outcome will be. Simply making a change to the SPACE, your ACTION or SKILL and leaving your THINKING on an out-of-date version, will NOT bring you the results you want. You would be unlikely to fully step in and commit to the outcome unless you also upgraded your THINKING and IDENTITY.

> The higher the level you make some change and adaptation, the more sustainable your outcome will be.

At the start of this chapter, I explained that most of what you do and think is a learnt response. Anything that is learnt can therefore be *un*learnt. Some people believe that changing your THINKING and IDENTITY is impossible or, at best, extremely difficult. It's certainly possible though I can't guarantee you it will be easy. Who wants easy anyway? I never said extraordinary was easy. In fact I have worked hard to show you that the opposite is true – being extraordinary takes a massive amount of energy, desire and discomfort. Believe me, if any of the things you needed to do to become extraordinary were easy, you would have done it by now and would have no need for this book.

I first learnt about the work of Robert Dilts about 15 years ago. To begin with, I wrestled with it as I found it complex and was unsure how I apply it. Then one day the light switch flicked on and it all made sense. Out of all the models, theories and concepts I know, I always come back to this one when I am stuck and treading water. It offers some reflection and an immediate choice point. I ask myself this one question:

In order to achieve this thing in front of me, at what level does the most significant change need to take place?

It is no more complex than that. So as that question starts to become your new habit, you too will be able to spot where you need to tweak and upgrade. Whatever level you decide needs the greatest shove, will in turn affect every other level too.

Fiddle with the right level

I have talked about writing a book for five years or more. I would tell people how much I wanted to do it … yet nothing transpired. Was it that I didn't know how (SKILL) to write? That I didn't know what (ACTION) to write about? Was it that I didn't have the right environment (SPACE) to write in?

No! It was none of these. The misalignment came from high up the map. I didn't have the courage, belief or conviction of my message (THINK) to do it. I wasn't sure anyone would want to read it (THINK). I didn't believe I had the time (also THINK as this was about my confidence to prioritize time). I didn't see myself as an author (IDENTITY).

Learning new SKILLS and just taking the ACTION was not ever going to be enough for me to produce a book. In fact, it wasn't what I needed at all. It took me a while to iron out my disabling THINKING that was preventing me from writing.

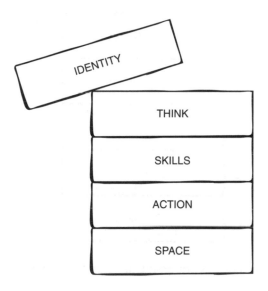

If I was to build this model out of wooden blocks as some kind of human Jenga, what do you think would happen if one level became massively misaligned from the others?

Of course, the structure would become unstable. And when it is unstable for too long, it collapses. This can happen to people too. If any level stays out of alignment for too long, you can quickly become unbalanced. The greater problem for you though, is not the risk of toppling over, but the risk of incongruence. I am pretty sure you will have met people throughout your life that tell you one story and yet act out another – we know that something is not quite right but can't necessarily put our finger on what it is. This is incongruence – the levels are misaligned.

The more aligned your levels can stay, the more congruent and aligned your messages will be. Each time you set an outcome for yourself, your team and your organization, check in with this map to see what needs to be in place at every level for your outcome to become your reality.

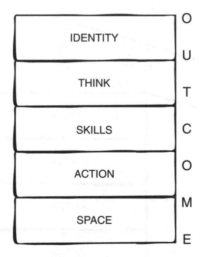

Throughout this book, I am going to refer to the Performance Map a great deal so that it becomes imprinted in your mind. Every Jolt I offer up will require you to consider at what level you need to make some adaptation for you to start dabbling with extraordinary.

Extraordinary is a way of being and thinking, not just a behaviour!

I am not a betting man, and if I was I could safely say that the ACTION level alone is not the blocker to you becoming extraordinary. What I see consistently with the leaders that I work with is that their lack of courage and confidence, their disabling beliefs and their out-of-date THINKING is what keeps them stuck.

★ Over to You

You have been invited to start looking through a new lens. You have been challenged to take a long hard look in the mirror. You have been offered a model that will clearly define where *you* need to focus if you are genuinely set on kicking ordinary into touch.

The better outcomes that you want for yourself, your team and your organization are within reaching distance if only you stretch out your THINKING enough and start taking some *new* ACTION.

The Jolts are ahead on the next page.

Before you get to them, what are you going to go and do differently right now, that will pave the way for the extraordinary road ahead?

Time to T-D-A.

THINK – DECIDE – ACT!

Part 2
The Jolts!

'Follow the instructions, no matter how abstract or impractical they may, at first, appear to be. The time will soon come, if you do as you have been instructed, in spirit as well as in action, when a whole new universe of power will unfold to you.'

Napoleon Hill, Think and Grow Rich.

Jolt 1
Choose well

Being extraordinary requires you to be accountable and responsible for your actions. It means leaving behind a culture of blame and starting to recognize the way in which you contribute to the outcome. Teams, organizations and cultures that are made up of individuals who own the part they play and choose their reactions will have far more extraordinary moments than ordinary ones.

1982 was when it all began. I was 10 and my mum took me to see Michael Crawford in the musical Barnum. I was totally awe-struck from start to finish, and in a random flash of inspiration I decided that I wanted to sing. Up to that point I had not once entertained the idea of singing or performing, however I took the rather bold step of auditioning for the school choir – after all, everyone gets in to the school choir. Don't they? Well, it didn't all go to plan as my music teacher, Mrs Jones, informed me that I had not made it into the choir this time – 'the singing thing isn't really for you Richard'. How unreasonable I thought, my voice sounds really good inside my own head …

I auditioned for a local musical group that was staging a production of Oliver. I went in, did my song, smiled cutely and left. I was convinced I had done enough. That was until the call arrived to say that despite my looking cute, 'singing may not be for him …'. Ok, ok, I get it, AND I STILL WANT TO SING! It is not difficult to spot that there was a big problem here – I wanted to be a singer yet the audience was making it quite clear that this may not be the best path for me to tread.

At 14 my voice broke and I went from sounding like a ropey boy soprano to a ropey baritone. Anyway, I coerced my parents into paying for me to have some singing lessons. The pieces started to fall in to place. Over the next three years I worked my butt off to develop my technique and my voice. Every spare moment was dedicated to improving. I found myself getting parts in amateur shows and my school productions and it felt as though the tide had turned. When I hit 17 I decided that the only college

I wanted to study at was Guildford Conservatoire – choosing to audition for just one college was high risk in such an overcrowded profession of wannabes! But that's what I chose and somehow I managed to blag myself a place. I had the most extraordinary three years there: rich in learning, rich in opportunity but generally not rich in cash. During my time I was given the most amazing parts to play and left with a brilliant agent to represent me. Stardom was surely just around the corner ...

When I left Guildford, I genuinely believed I was the next musical God, waiting for the world to hoover me up and lavish me with praise. I would take the world by storm and be paraded alongside the world's musical greats; Pavarotti, Elton John, Abba (ok, debatable) and Richard Tyler ... Why am I telling you all this? It's important because, as you'll soon see, this was the run up to a massive, greasy, walloping Jolt that was heading straight for me ... I just didn't spot it at the time. Be warned, some of the best Jolts that reach you will be the unexpected ones!

I started trawling the audition circuit thanks to my agent who helped open doors for me. I sang for the biggies; Miss Saigon, Phantom, Les Miserables, Starlight Express, Joseph, Cats ... do you know how many of those jobs I was offered? Yep. Zilch. Zero. Nada. Zip. There was a very good reason for all of this ...

My first audition and I found myself landed with the worst accompanist EVER to grace the planet. I had explained clearly to him exactly what I needed. Despite that, he did his own thing and made a real hash of it. I sang well. He played badly. I left the audition in the stroppiest diva state I knew. I got a call from my agent the following day to say, 'Not this time Richard ...'.

My next audition, I was admittedly a little late for. I got stuck on the train that happened to be terribly delayed. I arrived late and out of breath. I tried to justify myself but the panel were not interested. What could I do? 'I don't drive the trains', I explained. How could I have possibly played any part in the trains being late? I sang for them anyway – it was ok and didn't rock their world. I got a call from my agent the following day, *'Not this time Richard ...'*.

Now, my hair was long at the time and I rather unluckily happened to get caught in a downpour on my way to an audition. When I arrived, I looked like a Hungarian Puli (Google it and you'll know what I mean ...). For a 22-year-old, desperately trying to be cool, it was not a good look. If you're thinking of it at anytime as a potential career enhancer, avoid it. Anyway, I clearly didn't look like leading man potential despite singing nicely. They obviously couldn't see past the frizzy ball of mess and I got a call from my agent, the very next day to say, *'Not this time Richard ...'*.

Now, you will know what I mean when I say that sometimes in life we just happen to stumble into a run of bad luck. I'm sure you will have had a similar experience where it feels as though the universe is ganging up on you. Well, that's where I happened to find myself. You know what it's like; stuff happens to you and there is nothing you can do about it. After all, it is clearly not your fault ... right?

My agent called me with my next audition, a chance to sing for the West End production of Les Miserables. This was my calling. The moment where I could finally show off my talents and get my break. I arrive on time, hair looking good, voice working well and I am ready to rock it. I glance across the stage to the audition pianist ... S**T! Unbelievable. It would have to be wouldn't it?! Yes, the very same accompanist from my first audition. Sadly I didn't notice my massive choice point here – be charming and engaging or bully and blame? I instantly went for the latter, without even a fleeting consideration for the alternative. I was abrasive, abrupt, judging, disinterested and had turned my hearing right off so that I was not able to listen to his response ...

I took to the middle of the stage – I did my thing, he did his thing, and it was sadly NOT the same thing. I don't do angry much in life and this was one of those rare occasions where I excelled at it! You know the rest … I got a call from agent the next day to say, *'Not this time Richard …'*.

Imagine being in my map of the world at that very moment. All that I had dreamed of, hoped for, worked hard at, thrown back at me. I was confused. People even handed me the ladder to the pedestal for goodness sake, and I took my place on it, so why was I continually being rejected in situations that were clearly NOT MY FAULT? I expressed this all in less than charming terms to my agent. He took it and we eventually hit a moment of silence …

'Richard … SHUT UP. Just for one moment. SHUT UP. Stop. Listen. Think. Get your head out of your arse just for one minute. After that, you can shove it right back up there if you like. For now though, listen …'

He did certainly get my attention. Who speaks to their clients like that …?

'All I hear from you is blame. Nothing is ever your fault is it? You blame the pianist, you blame the people that drive the trains, you blame God for his weather choices, you blame your hair, the audition panel for not choosing you, me for not getting you the right auditions, you blame the day of the week that it is, the acoustics in the theatre, the temperature, your new shoes, the curry you had last night … you blame everyone and everything EXCEPT yourself …

The silence felt like a lifetime …

'Richard, I'll offer you one piece of advice. Do what you will with it. I have always lived by the idea of "It's not what happens TO you, it's what YOU CHOOSE to do about it" – It's not actually about the pianist, the weather, your hair, me, the temperature … it's only about the way YOU CHOOSE to react. However, you make it about all those things and by doing so take no responsibility or accountability for the outcomes. The easy solution is to go and have more singing lessons as that must be the reason you are not getting the jobs. Wrong. We often fix things by

upping our skills. But Richard, you sing well. You don't need to improve your technique; you just need to improve your attitude.'

I will never really know how much this conversation changed the course of the events that followed. Maybe if my agent hadn't been brave enough to call it with me and offer me that Jolt, I would still be carrying around the blame and telling the world how great I could have been if it wasn't for that terrible accompanist, terrible weather, unreliable train drivers …

It took me some time to process that conversation. Maybe I didn't want to. Sometimes people resist feedback not because they don't believe it is true or valuable but because if they take it on board, the expectation is set that they own it and will therefore act on it. To be honest, I didn't know what to do. I had gone through life, perhaps like you, believing that if something isn't working, then I needed to learn to be better at it – get more skills and practise harder. However, as I shared with you in Part 1, it is rarely just new skills that make the difference, as without the Jolt in THINKING, the skills alone don't stack up.

> It's not what happens TO you, it's what you CHOOSE to do about it …

What I did next was not rocket science. I started looking closer. I paid more attention to what I wanted and the way in which I was contributing to the outcome. I removed my head from my backside and started to spend time with my radar switched on. I began connecting with the world around me. I consistently asked myself two questions that became game changers:

How can I contribute to this outcome in the most positive way possible?

And after the event …

In what way did I contribute to that positively? What will I do differently next time?

As you now begin to do this, you will become accountable for your THINKING and your ACTIONS. This will allow you to check for necessary upgrades in advance and review your learning afterwards. So simple. Yet so extraordinary.

★ Over to You

I want you to stop now and turn down the volume on your inner noise. Find a quiet space where you can focus on this only.

It is easy to view any issue as being about the thing that *happened to you*; it was the other driver, your partner, your manager, your team, the culture, the day of the week …

Now think about one of the upgrades that you have chosen to make – where are you currently stuck blaming someone else or something that happened to you?

For you to make that upgrade, ask yourself this: how can you now take responsibility and choose to react differently? In what way do you now need to THINK about it, DECIDE what to do and then take ACTION that will Jolt the outcome?

Begin to T-D-A.

Jolt 2
Dare to begin before you are ready

'Let's hold off until we have complete buy in. We shouldn't really make any decision until we know that it is the right way to go. We can't afford to get this wrong so how about we spend some more time shaping it before we launch the idea …'

Inertia breeds ordinary and, in turn, ordinary ensures the inertia stays locked in – it's a very dangerous pattern. There is no place for it in your extraordinary performance. Bravery and your hunger to road-test ideas is what will see you building new habits that enable you to soar beyond ordinary …

How are decisions made in your organization? How much time and energy is invested in making sure that the idea is fail proof before you even dare to begin? How many moments do you spend thinking about the things you could do, imagining the most amazing outcomes and contemplating your next move ... yet failing to take any action whatsoever?

As you can imagine, the world of performance is a hot bed of creativity and ideas. Although those that enjoy the comfort of making a decision, taking action and then remaining fixed on that course will almost certainly struggle to fit in.

A few years ago, I was asked to take part in the workshop of a new musical production. A workshop gives the writer, director and producer the opportunity to see if the production works and if there is the potential for it to take a spot amongst London's other West End productions. There is huge vested interest in a venture like this as it can be the make or break of many careers. The company was chosen with care and we assembled for our first rehearsal. As with most workshops of this nature, the timeline is short and the expectation is enormous. All eyes are on you. Time is of the essence and with just eight days rehearsal time, we had a performance to give. Ordinary was not an option.

Ideas flowed, almost to the point of drowning in them. Each one was taken, given some time, and either discarded or tested. There was no time for navel gazing and deep contemplation. The only way to know if the idea had legs was to give it a go. All of the company were comfortable working this way. Well, all apart from one. Let me introduce you to Michael – he seemed to have an altogether different way of processing ideas that didn't quite connect with the other 12 people in the rehearsal space.

Imagine the situation – we were each responsible for inventing and exploring fresh ideas. The only true way to see if they were useable of course was to test them out and see what bounced back. Being able to spot if an idea might be the one to run with doesn't actually take that long, especially when you are immersed in a company of performers offering rapid-fire feedback and observation.

Michael's take was very different. What he wanted to do was to unpick each idea, question it, understand the rationale, discuss how it could fit and seek a consensus first, before even launching into exploration. Each time this happened, the energy dropped off. We stopped and thought about it. Thought some more. Debated his questions. And then thought some more. The vibrancy of the creative souls in the room ebbed away. It was as though the mood and energy were hoovered up in an instant. It was exhausting. We plummeted from a great creative height, smashed to the floor, before needing to drag ourselves back up again.

The result of all this was that we quickly stopped testing. We stopped daring. We talked more and played less. We began to question the play, our courage and our own abilities. Michael's power went viral. It seemed like we just soaked it up.

We had lost the courage to dare ourselves to begin ...

Each day you are faced with a constant stream of choices: a decision to be made, an idea to be embraced and an opportunity to be seized. But how do you know which ones to test out? How do you know whether to take on the role of Michael and to question, probe and think, or whether it is one of those moments that requires you just to step in and test it out?

> The answers and solutions are out there waiting to be discovered if only you will dare yourself to begin.

This is not about being a maverick or having a 'Gung ho' mentality to all that you tackle. As with everything in this book, the solutions are not digital: it is not simply a case of do this or don't do this. The answers sit on your own analogue dial; you can turn them up and turn them down. So the kick up the backside I am giving you is to spend more time choosing and then acting. The approach that Michael takes is genius ... but only when it helps to deliver an extraordinary outcome. The problem is when it becomes a habit, the default way and the only way. This is when opportunities to be extraordinary are bypassed.

There is such a pace and momentum to life that spending too much time attempting to form the perfect plan before launch can be a high-risk strategy. I have watched organizations contemplate launching the most astounding initiatives across their culture that could have ignited a tremendous buzz for their audience. The opportunity to deliver extraordinary outcomes was within their grasp, but the senior team decided to sit on it ... ponder ... question it ... seek consensus ... squabble over the perfect way forward, and whilst all that was happening the excitement dropped off, the door shut and their competitor nabbed the idea. They eventually got the Jolt and the learning, but only once they spotted that their competitor had taken the idea to market. The outcome could have been so very different if only they had dared to begin ...

★ Over to You

What are you currently sitting on but are too afraid to begin?

Perhaps it's a presentation, a piece of feedback you need to give, the question you need to ask or the flame you need to ignite?

What's stopping you? What's the risk in beginning now? Perhaps more importantly, what's the risk in waiting for the perfect moment to appear?

You have to kick it off. Once you start, you will begin to see solutions, connections and will then gather the insight you need to drive it forward.

Go on … I dare you.

Jolt 3
Take care of the small stuff

Being extraordinary requires a combination of getting the bold, brave and world-rocking vision in place whilst refining and tinkering with the small pieces. Beware of letting go of the small nuggets. Build a culture where everyone plays a role in tweaking and upgrading. Make it a consistent part of how you do business and you will find you build an audience that comes back to you, confident that you will deliver something extraordinary.

During a rehearsal for Les Miserables, I recall the Musical Director spending almost 20 minutes labouring just one solitary note with us. It seemed bizarre and unnecessary at the time. In a three-hour spectacle, why polish one note? One brave soul decided to ask the question that the rest of us were thinking;

'Why are we spending so long on one note that only lasts about nine seconds …?'

'Good question. There's an easy answer. We are investing the time so that we don't just get a good round of applause at the end but we get the audience up on their feet!'

Only then did it make sense. Take care of the tiny pieces that can have a significant effect on the outcome. That tiny tweak to a nine-second note did indeed get an audience to its feet. It was astonishing. There was no massive change to the note, the number of singers or the key in which we sang it. It was much simpler than that; we tidied the edges, had a different intention behind singing it and created a new warmth within the note. No rocket science involved. Just a small tweak that made an ordinary note extraordinary.

I am lucky enough to work with many organizations around the globe. Each year I get to touch thousands of leaders through the talks I give, the workshops I run and the people I coach. I observe one consistent theme – most of these people are overwhelmed. Working to the limit of their capacity with little head-space, yet their customers and the business continue to demand more. So, how can you and your organization ever progress if people are maxed out?

> Think about doing things *differently*, not about doing more!

What's it like in your team and your organization? How much capacity do people have for delivering more? When I first meet many of my new clients, they seem to be in an under-energized state where they express how they are trying hard to tackle monstrous goals alongside all the other boxes they have to tick as part of their Business as Usual approach. And they wonder why they are struggling …

One degree of change is a simple nugget that will revolutionize your life. It has transformed the way most of my clients approach their business, yet at face value is so simple. They have used it to make sweeping adaptations to the ways in which they think and act.

Here's how it works. A mathematician did a very simple sum. If you take two parallel train tracks and shift one of them by simply 1°, then 50 miles down the line the two tracks will be around 1 mile apart. Imagine that – the tiniest tweak by one degree can leave the two tracks a mile apart. Mindbending – how can a shift that is barely visible create such an impact down the line?

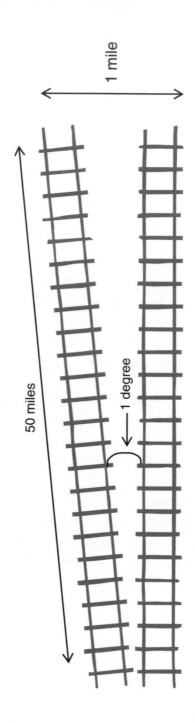

1 mile

50 miles

1 degree

How often do you attempt to make 180° changes that are all-singing and all-dancing because you believe they will deliver extraordinary outcomes? In many instances it is overwhelming and most people end up doing nothing! When you are brave enough to get in the moment, look closely, and then make consistent small tweaks, you can have the most astounding effect down the line.

Back in the rehearsal room, that tiny tweak to a nine-second note made a tremendous difference for both the audience and the performers.

This is not to say that you shouldn't have big, fat, hairy outcomes – you need those. And you will be most likely to make them a reality by consistently shifting 1° at a time. Over the last five years of rippling out 1° thinking across my clients, I have seen a theme appear – everyone can engage with making small tweaks. I have been a part of many heavy duty meetings where tasks are dumped on people and an expectation of a 90° shift in action is set. The following week, do you think the outcome had moved? Of course not. But people will have a good excuse or rationale and will often blame the thing that happened to them that meant they stopped focusing on the 90° outcome.

By changing the way that the outcome is set up, people can choose to react to it differently. Imagine what would happen if you were to ignite action in this way:

'I need each of us to work towards moving this outcome forward by just 1° over the coming week – We each need to take the tiny nugget, that will make a difference and move it forward – let's hear from everyone, what you will do to contribute to that?'

This frame creates possibility. It shows that we all play a role in contributing to the outcome. It encourages everyone to put their commitment out there in the room and, in most instances, people will easily dance with

1°. After all, 1° is nothing! As soon as 1° has been delivered, then we can move on to the next degree … and the next … and so on.

Test it out at your next meeting, I dare you!

★ Over to You

1° of change will very rapidly become a habit and a part of your everyday language. Once it has, it will then become a consistent part of your action.

How will you apply 1° thinking now? What one thing in your life will you improve by 1° today?

If you are genuinely driven to achieve extraordinary things, you will need to take action now.

How will you give an extra Jolt to your upgrades, by making a 1° shift?

I can't make you take action, that's up to you. I will, however, continue to prod, tickle and cajole until you do.

Jolt 4
Change feedback to *feedforward*

Imagine a time in the future when in your organization there is a constant stream of dialogue that encourages development. A place where people feel free to share their views, comments and challenges. A culture where the tough conversations are both offered and invited.

For me, this is the oddest Jolt in the book. Hmmm – not odd in a weird, peculiar kind of way – odd because of the learning that sits at the heart of it. In the deepest depths of the Artful approach, this Jolt is the most basic habit of the lot – it is so inherent, it nestles right at the top of the Performance model around THINK and IDENTITY. In fact, it is such a basic part of extraordinary performance that it would be easy to overlook it as being too simplistic. However, it is rarely viewed in quite the same way within organizational and team culture.

What I am referring to typically goes under the guise of 'feedback'. In some organizations I know, feedback is a swear word and even the slightest mumbling of it will bring instant dismissal to the culprit. Ok, I'm joking about that bit. However, for many people, even the mention of feedback brings a strong gut reaction; an emotional flooding of the body. I once suggested that I might give some feedback to a client many years ago – she was sitting right in front of me at the time, just she and I in the room. Instantly she started to shake, put her hand up to cover her mouth before beginning to cry. I was staggered at the reaction. I know people think I can be scary, but with this particular lady we had worked together well so far. So why such a strong reaction? She told me that she associated feedback with criticism, judgement and someone else's desire to undermine her. With that as her belief, there was little chance of the feedback I was about to give her landing in any way.

Sadly, this is not an unusual reaction in the business world. I see it often.

I'm curious …

How much feedback do you give? How much do you seek?

What's the general reaction in your organization to the idea of feedback?

How comfortable are people offering and receiving feedback?

What kind of feedback culture do you have within your team?

A feedback loop is forever present within the world of the arts: your audience will offer it to you constantly, your director, your musicians, the press, your colleagues and yourself as you gaze into the mirror.

In my head it's a very simple equation:

Feedback + Receptivity = Choice which = Possibility – this will lead you to Extraordinary.

Take away the feedback and what are you left with? Ordinary. Plain, old, ordinary.

> Extraordinary moments are created by a willingness to share your opinions and to welcome the opinions of others.

I think feedback can be a clumsy term. It is retrospective. It is rooted in what has been and not what is ahead. It can easily be loaded with judgement. Being extraordinary is about moving towards an outcome, and therefore the dialogue to make that happen also needs to be progressive and constantly nudging *forwards*, not *backwards*. After all, you cannot change what has been, only what is yet to come. Right?

Let me share something with you that will shift your view on this and allow you to flip your language on its head.

Feedforward – offering suggestions and insight for how to move forward, by making positive changes to THINKING, SKILLS and ACTION.

This simple Jolt has revolutionized many of the teams that I work with. It has transformed the way people engage with each other and elevated the way they offer insight and invite the views of others.

Here's how it works and some thoughts on how you can take it and apply it right now:

1. It is far more useful to help people learn to be 'right' than to prove they were 'wrong'. This can become such a waste of energy and yet is what happens much of the time with the giving of feedback.
2. I have seen numerous successful leaders resist any idea of feedback – however, I have seen the very same people embrace feedforward as they view it as something that is both helpful and developmental.
3. Whereas feedback can become slow and lumbering, drawing attention to faults and mistakes, feedforward can be delivered with some pace and energy.
4. In theory, feedback needs to focus on the 'behaviour and not the person' – in reality, this is rarely the case. Even if feedback is given brilliantly, it can still be personalized and received as an attack at IDENTITY level.
5. Feedforward needs to be delivered judgement free and with good intent – by that I mean offer it to the other person because you want them to have the chance to develop and improve. If you are simply pissed off with them, that is more your problem than theirs!
6. I frequently see that feedback re-enforces a negative cycle and people end up getting more of exactly what they didn't want! Feedforward enhances a positive cycle. It draws attention to what is wanted rather than what is unwanted.

7. Feedback can draw people into a game where the rules are more about 'let me get ready to respond to this comment' without fully taking the time to listen first. Feedforward, on the other hand, tends to get people listening far more as they believe they are going to receive something beneficial.

The Artful approach is loaded with feedforward: the constant stream of dialogue that is focused on moving forward and discovering new ways to do things. It keeps momentum and ensures the goal continues to be one of discovering the extraordinary.

Imagine if feedforward was a part of the story within your team …

How much closer would you edge towards extraordinary?

Think how much simpler it would be to offer and invite high quality input.

This Jolt feels like the right place to be offering you a bonus Jolt: 2 for the price of 1!

Based on the principle of 'mood goes viral' – what if you were to spend more time noticing and recognizing glimmers of extraordinary?

Spotting the MOBs.

Spotting the Moments of Brilliance!

I recently worked with a team from an International Law firm where they took on the habit of feedforward. Their team dynamic quickly elevated. When the people became engaged in the idea of MOB-ing, they recognized the need to spend more time being present with their radar on. People soon saw the ease with which they could offer a MOB to someone that they worked with. The payoff though was watching the response and then seeing how the mood that was created quickly spread – the effect of the MOB was passed on. For a team that had historically been stuck in the past, blaming each other for every mistake, this was quite a turning point.

Sometimes we can be all too quick to spot the MOCs – the Moments of Crap!

The problem with this is that they too will go viral and the mood will quickly ripple out.

You need to decide where to spend your attention – MOCs or MOBs?

> ## ★ Over to You
>
> Take some time to consider how much of an honest dialogue you contribute to. How open is your team to sharing and receiving insights?
>
> How would it be different if this were to improve by just 1°?
>
> Where can you start to introduce feedforward? I dare you to begin the ripple: set the frame for the principles of feedforward first.
>
> Then kick it off – 'Here are three ideas for things to do differently to propel you forward …'
>
> Hand out some MOBs today – spot the Moment of Brilliance and pass it on.
>
> This quality of the dialogue will be a lever for the ordinary to extraordinary transformation.
>
> You gotta be brave though to get it moving …

Jolt 5
Dare yourself to fail

'Oooh, not too much ... no, not like that ... this way ... careful not to drop it ... make sure we don't lose this one ... that will cost you your job if you get it wrong ... that's too risky so better play it safe ... make sure you don't forget to tell him ... but what if I forget the words ... and if the music doesn't play, I'll look really silly ...'.

Convincing ourselves and others that it is best to get it right each time will come at the ultimate price: a lack of daring, stifled creativity and the delivery of something mindnumbingly ordinary!

'Failure is good. Big failure is better. Big, ignominious failure in front of a lot of people is the best.'

Erik Kessels

I love that quote! I am sure that it may well send a few shudders through you. It's pretty bold. It also gives a strong insight into the attitude of Erik Kessels and how he runs his own business. Erik set up an über-cool ad agency in Amsterdam and now has offices in LA and London. His business is founded on the notion of daring to make mistakes. In fact, he goes one step further than that and actively encourages the art of making mistakes, believing that mistakes open the doors to new opportunities. He even runs workshops on the principles of 'Forced Errors' – facilitating ways to actively make mistakes. How cool is that?!

You can be forgiven for thinking that both myself and Erik have completely lost our minds. To many, it does indeed appear that way.

I'll let you into a secret. When I had greatest mastery of being a perfectionist – or when the perfection had the greatest mastery over me – I spent many hours asking myself one question:

'What if I fail?!'

Have you ever asked yourself that … on constant repeat?

If rehearsed enough, this can become one of the most disabling and destructive questions you can ask. Mine ran on auto play – it just kept on looping round and round. The more I asked it, the more I managed to embellish my own answer and create a mini Armageddon in my head. The consequence being that I managed to talk myself out of doing anything new and ensuring that my courage and bravery to push at the edges was redundant. I made the perceived risk seem so big, that I became paralysed and this resulted in me deciding that ok was, after all, ok. In fact ok was just ordinary.

Most of the Jolts are to help you change habits and ask the uncomfortable questions that provoke you to choose a different way. You will soon start to become even better at choosing between the habits that are working and the ones that are old school. Having that gut feeling that prompts you to ask the question 'What if I fail?' can be a useful voice to listen to, but NOT if it is the only question you ask – NOT if it is dominant and NOT if it is no longer asked by choice, but simply runs as the default question.

I actually believe that the answer to the question in hand is very simple.

'What if I fail?'

The answer?

You will!

Yep, that's right, you will. You will screw it up, you will make a mistake and you will sing plenty of bum notes along the way.

There is a much healthier and progressive place to put your attention and energy. Once you have asked yourself the question and listened to the answer, move onto something more liberating and ask yourself this:

'Once I have failed and got it wrong, what will I do next to get 1° closer to extraordinary?'

You see the thing is, once you have failed and ONLY once you have failed will you open the possibility for an outcome that could rock the world. Getting it wrong will deliver you vast insight and knowledge that, in most instances, will only be visible once you have danced with failure.

'Test fast, fail fast, adjust fast.'

Tom Peters

Some intelligence and thinking is required here. As a leader you have responsibility to make decisions that enhance and grow the business – a massive part of that is the courage to get things wrong and the bravery needed to allow others to do the same.

You also have a moral obligation to make the right decisions in alignment with the culture and ethos of the organization. Having a 'who gives a s**t if I fail' attitude is not a get out of jail card that encourages illegal or morally wrong decisions to be made.

Daring to fail requires resilience. Let's face it, many of the things that you test out will not work in the way that you had planned. I'm sorry to have to tell you that. You will get something and perhaps it will be a long way off from what you wanted.

The words, 'Go on, I dare you to screw it up' seem to trickle out of my mouth on a fairly regular basis. If I'm working with a leadership team, some feathers are ruffled to start with. The immediate reaction from a few will be: 'Ha, what does he know about our business – there's no space for us to fail.' And that is a part of the problem. Once a belief has become fixed like that, it becomes a part of the day-to-day story and language. However, after these comments are shared around, it doesn't take long before a very different mood goes viral. People start to see others daring. They notice that a few others in the room are testing out ideas, getting it wrong, receiving feedback, rallying together to find the next way and then forging ahead. Importantly, they see that their performance improves as a result of screwing up.

Before you know it, this new mood will go viral.

> Performance can improve, only when you start to screw up!

Organizations will stagnate unless the hunger for learning and the daring to fail ticks away consistently at both the THINKING and ACTION level. Even a 1° lean towards some conscious daring will make a significant difference.

★ Over to You

How much do you dare yourself to fail? Be honest.

How often do you encourage an attitude of daring to fail amongst your team?

What gets in the way?

Look, I'm not saying go through life with your eyes shut making random decisions. That's plain stupid.

I am challenging you to build an attitude where daring to fail, daring to take all the learning and daring to get the next idea moving, becomes the norm. That way you will harness a sense of continual growth. And whilst your competitors sit still, determined to play it safe, you will be leaping ahead.

What will you dare to do now ...?

Jolt 6
Veer from the routine and get wonky

You know what ordinary is like: safe, magnolia, nice, plain and does the basics. Comfortable too. A straight, balanced and unwavering delivery approach will pretty much guarantee this. Those that strive to stand out, be noticed and add a burst of colour to the world will play an alternative strategy. They will spend more time shaking things up, testing out more new ideas and daring to get it wrong more often. The likes of Apple and Innocent spend far more time on the wonk than your average ordinary organization. Time to get wonky then …

had completed my first year at Guildford Conservatoire where I was studying Music and Theatre. I thought it had been a resounding success. I had got the lead role in the end of year show and had worked my butt off to be really *good*. Seemingly though, that was the problem.

At the close of each term, every student had a review meeting: a chance for the teaching faculty to share their thoughts. This was my first proper foray into some rather hardcore feedback. I sat down, faced with the Principal, the Head of my course and a few other key members of staff. I waited for them to hose me down with praise and adoration …

The reality was slightly different from how I had imagined it. They told me they thought I was good, nice, reliable, neat, tidy and consistent. Bingo I thought! I smiled, punched the air and looked generally smug.

'No Richard. Good won't survive here and good won't survive in this business – we need you to show you are better than that. There is not enough work out there for everyone so being good won't be good enough. There are loads of good singers and good actors. How do you expect to stand out if you are just good? You need to show us you have more than that. You need to shake things up over the summer break. We expect to see a new and improved Richard in September.'

I was dumbfounded. I had been doing so well and had worked hard for that. No one had criticized 'good' before. My experience up to that point was one of being actively encouraged by my teachers, my parents and my friends to 'be good'. I always tried to be my best. I had some weird hunger for perfection – my 'be perfect' driver was off the scale. In so many ways, that was the problem. My drive to be perfect stopped me from being bold, brave and bucking the trend.

Later that day, as I packed my bags to leave the rehearsal room, the Head of Drama caught me. He was a sprightly and energetic director full of wisdom and passion. When he spoke, people listened. He bounded over. 'Richard, it's really quite simple. No need to be confused by the feedback. You're good. That's a fact. However, good is not enough in this business. All you need to do is *get a bit wonky.* Really, it's that easy ...' And off he skipped.

Get wonky? What?! I raced after him. 'Now I'm really confused, what am I supposed to do with *get a bit wonky*?'

'Richard, you play it safe every time. I don't ever see you get it wrong. I don't see you risk yourself. Whatever you do is nice, precise and pleases people. Unless you unleash something else from within, you will never be your best. Be brave, push to your edge, take a risk, screw it up, crack a note, dare yourself, forget your words, make a mistake, look scruffy. By daring yourself to get it wrong, you will learn most. You have such rigid boundaries that you have trapped yourself. Only by getting on the wonk will you find your own edge and have some chance of discovering what extraordinary is like.'

As yet another jolt walloped me, the penny dropped ...

I had convinced myself that perfect = playing safe. If only I could make it work every time, be consistently good and for my audience to say, 'yes, he's nice ...' then I would be sorted.

How far off track is that from creating anything remotely extraordinary?

How far off track are you from creating extraordinary experiences for yourself and your audience? When have you done the same deal with yourself and are now left delivering something nice, good and, at best, ordinary?

Just imagine that you made a decision, right now, that your mantra was to be *get wonky.* Ultimately, of course, it's my mantra but if you're really interested, I'll lend it to you! Please hand it back in pristine condition once you are done …

How would you run your day differently? Remember, the Performance Map from Part 1 clearly demonstrated that the higher the level you make the change, the more sustainable the outcome will be. This requires you to upgrade your THINKING first, before taking new ACTION.

Getting wonky is not about being wacky for the sake of it. Getting wonky is an attitude where the driver is all about increasing audience experience and engagement. I want to be clear with you about the purpose of getting wonky, otherwise I fear you may start wearing pink trousers, Hawaiian shirts and adopting a funny walk – apologies if you already do those three things! Look, as consumers we are bombarded by the good and the ordinary. We drown in mediocre offerings. It is the extraordinary that grabs our attention.

Once you have caught the attention though, you still have to deliver on it. It is about standing out. It is about you being brave enough to be different enough!

Getting wonky is NOT about being wacky for the sake of it. It is about you pushing at the edges to stand out in a world that is flooded with magnolia!

Adopting the wonky approach invites you to ask 'What if?' and 'Why not?' before deciding what to do, as opposed to just running a 'We always do it that way' script. It means taking more risks and THINKING and ACTING in a more playful way. All of this builds an air of newness.

I sat in a client team meeting last month. It was one of their weekly turgid information-sharing sessions where people went through the motions, ticked the boxes and then went back to sleep. It took the bravery of one soul to jolt the entire meeting. Alex is a newly promoted VP. I could see that he was plotting something as the creeping circle of death moved around the room. It was 45 minutes into the 60-minute meeting when he first spoke. He paused and made eye contact with every single team member before uttering a word …

'When I got home last night, my 6-year-old daughter had waited up for me. She had drawn me a picture that she was desperate to share. It looked like yet another drawing of some clouds, the sun, the sky, birds, people and trees. Nothing unusual. However, she went on to explain how it is that we are all connected. If we look up into the sky Daddy, we can see the sun or the clouds or the moon and the moment we do this, wherever anyone is in the world, we connect with them. We don't have to be next to them. We are all connected, all of the time. So when you go to America for work Daddy, I am still with you …

Pretty profound for a 6-year-old. So, as I sat here listening to each of us wading through our disconnected information, I thought a 6-year-old's wisdom might help. We are all connected. We are in this thing called a 'team', together. We take the hits and the successes, together. We only need look up to the sky and we are reminded how connected we are. Only if we work in a connected and joined up manner can we turn these issues around and start to delight our customers again. And that's what we are all here for, right?'

Silence ... before one of the team offered a resounding YES! Every single person in that room had just reconnected with the mission. More than what they said, their body language told a new story. They looked like a team with some power to spend as they sat upright and alert. They got it. Each one plugged in again. The final 15 minutes of the meeting generated more new thinking and energy from that team than I had ever seen from them.

The thing is, Alex went out on a limb to share that story. It was not his comfortable place. You would not describe him as an expert storyteller. He hadn't been on a course to learn how to do it. In fact, the easiest thing would have been for him to fit in, collude with the first 45 minutes and be ordinary. Instead, he spotted that something was not working, believed he needed to contribute, adapted his THINKING and followed up with some ACTION. He got wonky!

When have you had moments like Alex? Where did you veer from the routine in order to provoke a different outcome?

The most inspiring outcome of all this is not that Alex spends more time on the wonk, but that every member of the entire management team now acts out a different story. In their own unique way, each one gets a little bit wonky as they are focused on telling a new story. Get wonky is their mantra. How will you make it yours?

★ Over to You

Wonky is on a sliding scale. You can turn it up, or down, as necessary. It's not on or off.

Where in your life could you now turn up your wonky dial? Perhaps from a 3–4 or 6–7? Just by 1°…

If you feel really brave, share the Getting Wonky mantra with your team and encourage them.

The ACTION that you take will be easy to define. The stretch is building in the wonky THINKING first.

Decide on what you could do right now. Brave enough?

Then get wonking …!

Jolt 7
Know where you need to get to

*Where are you heading? What's your destination?
How will you know you have arrived?*

*People that make extraordinary things happen don't just
stumble across their success. They dream it. They see it. They
play it out in their own minds over and over again. Do you
think Mo Farah plays out his successes in his own mind before
taking the appropriate action? Yes! Do you think that Tom
Ford happens to trip over a design for a new suit every now
and then? No, of course not. Do you believe that J K Rowling
sat down to write Harry Potter without a single thought in
advance? No way.*

*Based on that, are you waiting for your extraordinary
performance to find you or are you out there hunting it
down...?*

'Red and yellow and green and brown and scarlet and black and ochre and peach ...'

I have the lyrics to the title song from Joseph and his Amazing Technicolour Dreamcoat locked away deep in my unconscious. I'm not proud of it you know. I just happen to have heard it a few times over the years. Well, that coupled with my 15 auditions for the part of Joseph in London ... which I didn't ever get, and the fact that I have taken my daughter to see the show too many times to mention. Anyway, it's locked in there. I can see it with absolute clarity. The soundtrack plays along at the same time in my head and I'm instantly there – starring as Joseph. The problem is I know that it is an outcome that will now never come to fruition, as who wants a 42-year-old Joseph?!

As a leader, and an extraordinary one at that, your outcomes and vision also need to be in bright technicolour. They need to be alive in your head; singing, dancing, sparkly lights and with surround sound. If they don't live with that clarity in your own mind, how the heck do you expect them to land with others? How will your team translate something that doesn't really come alive for them?

Outcomes matter!

I think it would be useful to start by telling you what Outcomes aren't.

Fantasies – Having fantasies can be good in life. We all need some fantasy. I won't share mine here, as they will be in the next book …! However, fantasies are NOT outcomes. They are dreaming without a plan and are rarely based in any sense of reality. I used to work for an organization where one of the directors relied solely on fantasies to run the business – 'We will dominate the world, we will be in everyone's head, everyone will want a slice of us …' I would spend my days totally tranced out, believing that if I just imagined hard enough, it would somehow manifest itself, as if by magic … Well, it didn't, ever.

Wish lists – These are the lesser version of a full-on fantasy. I hear conversations in teams that are based around: 'Oh I wish we could do that … I wish we could win him over … I wish we could have more resource … I wish we could work with her …' People collude, join in the wishing and, nothing happens … Just more wishing.

Plans – these are the 'how'. You will need plans. However, what good is a 'how' if you don't have the 'what' and the 'why'? I know 'how' to drive my car but if I don't have a destination, then I will just be faffing around.

Targets and objectives – These are your measures. These are also not to be confused with outcomes. If you focus on these alone, you are just fixating on tick boxes, numbers and metrics. The problem with this is also that it becomes hard to engage people around a common mission and story. I work with many Public Sector organizations that fixate over targets – people are totally wrapped up in delivering a number but with no idea why and what the greater purpose of that number is, apart from keeping someone else happy whose job it is to input the right numbers in the right boxes! Goodness, how exhausting.

Follow any of these paths and you can be sure you will stay kissing the cheek of ordinary. You don't want that though do you?

> Outcomes must be bold, brave and compelling – they must ignite passion – yours, and that of others.

Three years ago I was asked to appear in The Phantom of the Opera 25th anniversary production at the Royal Albert Hall; 125 performers were assembled as the dream cast. The production was to run for three performances only, be recorded to DVD, CD and beamed all around the globe to cinemas as a live feed. It didn't take me long to decide – YES PLEASE!

Our first day of rehearsal and we had a 15-minute introduction from Sir Cameron Mackintosh and Lord Andrew Lloyd Webber as to why they were doing this and the outcome they wished for it. You could hear a pin drop throughout. It was an inspiring and moving moment: 125 performers totally engaged in the vision and under no illusion as to what it was we needed to deliver. The Sir and the Lord had certainly spent many hours dreaming up what was required for this to be a truly extraordinary theatrical experience. They didn't need to know all of the 'how' – they did however have to have the 'what'. No fantasy, no wish lists and no targets – there was a plan, of course, as we only had 14 days to make their outcome a reality. No option to get lost in our heads as this was about delighting the audience. This was our Jolt, our call to adventure. And off we went …

So, how can you create an outcome of your own? Here goes. This is the only model you need. Use it for your big hairy life outcomes or the small nuggets you need to make happen during your day. Importantly, use it. THINK outcome.

1. What do you want?

So often we create our outcomes through knowing what we *don't* want. The problem with that is that you will end up getting exactly what you *don't* want! It's key that you get clear on what you DO want. State your outcome in the positive. Use positive language to describe what you will feel, have, think, see, do …

2. **Step in and imagine your new reality**

   This is the part of outcome shaping that many people miss out. Imagine that you now have this outcome – it's yours. What's it like – describe it. Use vivid and compelling language. Ensure you speak about it in the present tense: 'I am … I have … I see ….'

3. **How do you know?**

   This is where you gather evidence and feedback. How do you know it is what you want? How do you know it is what your audience wants? What are they telling you? What are you seeing around you that convinces you that you've arrived?

4. **Who's in the driving seat?**

   Do you have total control and ownership of making this outcome a reality? Yes? Excellent – onwards. No? So, who else do you need to get on board? Who will play a role in making this happen? How will you engage them and connect them with this idea?

5. **Things for the journey?**

   What resources do you need to make it happen: people, time, money, skills, equipment, space, jelly moulds? Get clear on all the important things that are required to make sure you are on track.

6. **Get into first gear!**

   You can only move forward once you're in first gear. In neutral, you go nowhere. You can build the best outcome ever and it's no good if you can't ship the idea and begin it. Get in first gear, dare yourself to start and then go. It only needs to be a 1° movement: the first phone call, arranging a meeting, signing up, booking on, checking in. Do it.

Muddling along in life, seeing where the path leads is a choice. You just need to be sure if it is a choice you make that will get you what you want. What it won't open up is the possibility that you move beyond ordinary and stare extraordinary in the face.

Making your outcome a reality takes persistence, rigour, precision and bloody hard work.

The extraordinary moments that are created in any art form are always born out of a compelling outcome: a vision that is so bright and so dynamic it sets the framework for the performers to breathe life into it.

The same is true with leadership. For you to inspire a team of people to leap towards extraordinary means that you need to present them with the meaningful outcome to start with.

★ Over to You

You will have outcomes, I'm pretty sure of that.

The question is: what outcomes do you now need to be setting for yourself that will edge you towards extraordinary?

Take some time to reflect on it. Pick one. Now work it through the outcome model.

Get your first step in place and take it …Outcomes will see you arrive in some extraordinary places. Brave enough to give it a whirl?

Jolt 8
Adopt your authentic posture

Extraordinary leaders will make an extraordinary impact. You will know when they are around. You will spot the congruence and alignment between their words, thinking and their action. You will see it through the way that they sit, stand, walk, make eye contact and shake your hand. Being extraordinary requires you to adopt the right posture to get the best outcome.

How do you currently use your posture to enhance your powers of extraordinary?

For many years we have been bombarded by various experts on both the covert and overt rules of body language; the ability to understand exactly what the twitching left eye means every time someone says the word harpoon …

'Hmmmmm, I noticed that his left eye twitches whenever he says the word harpoon … I wonder what that could mean …?'

What it means is this: NOTHING! He happens to say harpoon a lot and has an unfortunate twitch in his left eye. Now start paying attention to the nuances of body language and voice that tell you something useful!

You can tell I'm not a fan. Having an understanding of body language and being able to determine what the subtle messages might mean is certainly useful. However, there are massive generalizations at play and this is where we all need to take extra care. Applying a set of rules to everyone we meet and expecting those subtle messages to fit in a box is a waste of your time. I do absolutely believe that when you have a deep level of rapport with someone it is easier to spot the patterns of their non-verbal cues and that, at best, offers you an opportunity to question and seek greater understanding if the verbal and non-verbal cues appear not to be in harmony with the overall message. However, be careful not to see this as a free ticket that permits you to make an assumption about their motives and their thinking.

As you will have worked out already, this Jolt is not going to offer you the perfect body language formula of extraordinary folks. Firstly, it would be almost impossible to create that blue print, as there is no 'one size fits all' approach for being extraordinary. Secondly, being extraordinary needs both THINKING and ACTION that keeps you nimble and flexible: your ability to adapt depending on your outcome and your audience. In my eyes, this renders a body language rule book useless.

I regularly speak on the conference circuit, and I consider myself extremely fortunate to see some of the world's most extraordinary speakers and thinkers strut their stuff. I have been lucky enough to witness the likes of Graeme Codrington, Nancy Duarte, Matthew Syed, Geoff Ramm and Tony Robbins, amongst others. All of them so different and each one extraordinary. They are all able to form a unique and personal connection with every audience member, seducing them to listen to their message. Now, the thing is, do they all have some similar funny walks I can share with you? Do they have a funny head twitch that separates them from the ordinary? Is their posture a cloned version of each other's? No, no, no.

So then, what is it that marks them out from the other, more magnolia, speakers?

They share many qualities but what pervades most when they are on stage is their belief in themselves and their message. They are authentic – they are true to what they stand for. If you go back to the Performance model that we looked at earlier in the book, and shoot right to the top, you will find IDENTITY and THINK. I talked to you about the requirement in delivering anything extraordinary is to turn it from a task, at ACTION level, into something that you are, at IDENTITY level. What differentiates these speakers from the other ordinary speakers is not simply their ability, knowledge, skill and experience, it is that at IDENTITY level, they **are** speakers and communicators – remember, an IDENTITY statement will ripple down though every other level in the model. The messages that they share are delivered with strength and they are more definite in their delivery style. They present with courage and certainty. They deliver with conviction. No fluff. No buffers. No woolly padding around the edges. Just commitment to their thinking, their message and the impact that it will have on you, their audience.

> What sits at an IDENTITY level for you will ripple out into every other level; affecting your THINKING, SKILL, ACTION and the SPACE you are in.

Let me ask you a few questions about your IDENTITY then:

Are you a leader?

Are you a speaker?

Are you an entrepreneur?

Are you a catalyst for change?

... who are you?

I hear you asking: what has this to do with body language and adopting the posture? The answer is: everything!

The reality is that for every extraordinary speaker I have watched on stage, I have seen many that, at best, dabble with ordinary. The sad thing is, many of them seem to have great ideas, have had awe-inspiring experiences and do actually have a decent story to tell. They could easily ignite audiences and give them a Jolt, but it just doesn't happen.

So, what's missing? Conviction, commitment, courage and hunger to dare themselves. This leaks out through their tone of voice and the way they hold themselves – their posture. Because it's disconnected from their message, they lose their power and the audience never truly engages.

What can you do then to adopt the posture of someone that is extraordinary and make it a true fit for you?

You can begin by creating a movie in your mind of someone who is extraordinary and start bringing that movie to life.

Find somewhere comfy. Make sure you are in a frame of mind to be receptive and open to new ideas. Flick on the cinema in your mind and take your premium seat. On the screen in front of you, start playing the trailer for 'ME', the movie. This movie is full to the brim of all your extraordinary life moments – some you will have already lived out, others are just on the horizon! As it starts to roll, pay attention to:

The way you stand when you are grounded.

The way you move with purpose.

How you hold an extended moment of silence ...

The way you look with intention and conviction.

The way you take your place, centre stage.

How you stand, move and sit when you tackle the uncomfortable stuff.

How you physiologically change when moving from 'It's not what happens to you ...' to 'choosing to react in the most appropriate way ...'

Deep in the roots of the Artful approach is the ability to make a vision real inside your mind before it can become a part of your THINKING and ACTION. This is about forming something in your mind that is so clear, so bright and so very compelling. This takes constant rehearsal, tweaking and reviewing. There is no speedy route to bypass the work involved in this. Fortunately, within the power of your own mind is the biggest and fastest hard drive – you can record onto it, edit and delete.

Have you ever watched a really rubbish film? I mean REALLY rubbish? Perhaps one that you have switched off in the first five minutes? I have, lots! Would you ever then go back and watch it again and again and again? It's unlikely, right? I wonder how many terrible movies you run in your own mind that you do play over and over and over again? You know, the ones where you screwed up, looked a fool, tripped over, forgot your words ... you will have a vast collection I'm sure. Why store them? Why not replace them with something that enables you rather than disables you?

Once you begin to get your movie running that shows you at your most extraordinary, your THINKING and ACTION will start to follow suit, allowing your extraordinary posture to enhance your messages.

One of the realities of being human is that we are not going to be constantly on form. We have off days and extraordinarily super smashing great days. The difference between the ordinary moments and extraordinary ones is where you work hard to build in some additional super smashing great days! Perhaps you could start to T-D-A a bit more:

THINK ... DECIDE ... and then ACT!

★ Over to You

What does the extraordinary version of you look like?

Time to get active now and start running the movie that you just created.

By just 1°, seize the chance to upgrade your posture: choose a meeting that you have in the next two days.

Now decide on your outcome and the impact you want to have. At IDENTITY level, which extraordinary version of yourself are you taking to the meeting?

From way before you enter the room to way after you have left: increase your energy, hold the pause, move with greater purpose, be definite and connect with EVERY member of your audience.

Jolt 9
Unleash your real voice

He was a strong leader that his own team looked up to. As the new UK MD it was right that he fronted the next regional conference as people wanted to hear his views. They wanted to be a part of the journey and were ready to be led by him. The word had been out on the streets for months now that his crystal-clear vision and bold plans for future growth had legs. The 'new story' that so many had waited for was at last becoming their reality. The organization had spent a long time fiddling around being ordinary with dysfunctional leadership at the very top getting in everyone's way. This was the new beginning …

> **'One word expresses the pathway to greatness: voice. Those on this path find their voice and inspire others to find theirs. The rest never do.'**
>
> *Stephen R Covey*

The call came into me about four weeks before the regional conference. A rather desperate sounding HR Director was the one bold enough to reach out – 'We need you. You have to help us Richard. The new MD, Tony, is brilliant: a visionary … a transformer … but with no voice. Well, he obviously has a voice but we have just got him up to run through the conference launch and … well … it just didn't happen. He crumbled. The charisma he has with a small team was lost in such a big space. It's like he literally has NO voice. Can you weave some magic please? And quickly.'

I'll be honest; I love getting calls like this as I work well under pressure with tight deadlines. I feel like it gives me even more permission to Jolt and provoke. My experience also shows that amazing transformations can happen rapidly when we want them enough so I believed that the MD could make big leaps. Actually, it was non-negotiable. He HAD to.

The human voice is the most powerful and flexible instrument you could wish for, yet most people rarely explore its full potential in their lifetime.

The average human speaking voice has around 30 notes available to use – most people will fall into a pattern that sees them using somewhere between three and five notes.

How limiting, don't you think? Do you fall into that group? Can you imagine a concert pianist using only 10% of the keys? It just wouldn't happen.

I feel very passionate about the use of the human voice and recognize the massive potential that is lost by failing to take it to its edge. It's another book in itself! But for now, I want to give you enough of a wallop for you to make the relevant upgrade to your own voice.

Living an Artful approach has taught me so much in my life and enhanced what I do not only as a performer, but as a leader and a human being too. At the core of that, the work I have done on my voice has made the biggest difference by far. It has not only allowed me to express myself and 'have my say', it has presented me with a catalogue of ways to engage my audience.

> A voice that enhances, soothes, connects and invigorates is driven by the right THINKING that in turn provokes the most suitable ACTION.

Consider this for a moment – from birth, most people are blessed with the perfect vocal system. It's astounding how a small, perfectly formed cherub can be such an extraordinary vocal gymnast and unleash so much influence on the world around them. I remember being amazed on a daily basis by how my own daughter could express joy, hunger, fear, cold, heat, enjoyment, thirst, anger, frustration, sleep deprivation, triumph, panic, curiosity and such amusement at my jokes … with not a single word at her disposal. Not one word, yet her capacity to express all of those things with her voice alone was mind-boggling. Often she could continue for hours and hours on end with no sign of a sore throat. Just two parents with sore eardrums!

I find it awe inspiring that there is such capacity for sound and expression within a tiny, fragile human being. The question is though, where does it all go wrong? When does that capacity for expression get tucked away? What, for so many, becomes the blocker that stops that natural ability to express and connect through emotion?

I think the answer, in part, is the formation of language. Words begin to appear and replace the need for authentic expression of emotion and feeling. Why work to express an emotion when it is easier to use the words happy, sad, angry, upset ...? We all face this as we grow up. Our culture, environment and the beliefs and values lived out around us will determine just how much we each go on to align our language with the relevant emotion.

I occasionally ask the groups that I work with to use one word that describes the day they have just had with me – a young man, sat on the front row, exclaimed 'Excited – best day of my life!' – sadly, without the words, his voice told a different story; monotone, flat, no energy, slow. He could easily have been telling me that it was the 'worst day of his life'.

I laughed, the audience laughed and he laughed. We couldn't fail to notice that his message and his tone were not in sync. We chatted together after the session and despite the fact that he had had an awesome day, he recognized that he communicated it in the same way that he communicates most of his messages – he relies upon the words alone to convey the meaning and the emotion.

Just re-visit the Performance model from Part 1 of the book for a moment. It is highly unlikely that at an ACTION and SKILL level, you don't know how to use your voice well. You can, can't you? That is a different question to ARE YOU using your voice well! Ah, yes, you do need to practise to get all those 30 notes you have moving – of course, that goes without saying.

At a THINKING level though, what gets in the way of you using your voice in an authentic way?

What stops you fully expressing yourself and sharing what's on your mind?

Are you courageous enough to release your voice to convey greater emotion and meaning?

> How much more do you need to dare yourself in order to unleash your real voice?

Back to Tony who was in desperate need of help. During our first session, I had him up on his feet and delivering his opening messages for the conference. It was quite bewildering to witness a tall, strong, power-dressed leader express himself with a voice that can only be described as having been stolen from one of the organ mice in the 1970s children's programme, Bagpuss. It was bizarre; squeaky, thin and apologetic. Before he took to the stage, something switched off in his head that meant his natural ability to speak was pushed deep inside. We talked at length about his first senior leadership role almost 14 years prior to this point. He had stepped up to present to a group of board members who had ripped both his messages, and his style, to shreds. He still ran the movie like it was yesterday. Each time he watched it, it became clearer and more lifelike. It would dominate his thinking whenever he needed to speak to more than about 15 people. I decided that radical action was needed so that Tony could scramble his thinking. I wanted to distract him from *this* issue and offer him a *different* place to focus …

It wasn't long before I had him singing his presentation as an Opera Diva. It was at this point, I think, that Tony decided he didn't like working with me very much. What followed though was quite extraordinary, his THINKING upgraded, as the context had now changed and what his mind had been doing was no longer relevant. His old thoughts didn't work. In his head, he was just pretending and playing and believed that this wasn't real life. Ha. But of course it was real, just a new invention. What proceeded to erupt from his body was a rich, resonant and colourful sound. Tuneful? No, but that wasn't the outcome. The Outcome was a Jolt in thinking to bring about some expression and the use of his full voice. Ten minutes down the line and I asked him to sing a line and then immediately speak the same line with the identical ACTION and THINKING he used for singing it. Boom! He nailed it.

Look, I don't recount that story to sell my expertise as a coach and to show you I'm the bee's knees. No, I share it with you to demonstrate how fast a step change can be made when you become willing to dare.

The work with Tony evolved over the next few weeks: we talked lots, unwrapped out-of-date THINKING and planted some new ideas to build on. By the time the conference arrived he was almost giddy with excitement – it had been a long time since he had used his voice to connect both people and ideas. His vision at last crystallized and his audience were seduced.

Your voice is one of the most powerful connectors that you have. It opens up your own authenticity and persuades your audience to engage with you. Taking away that means of expression and storytelling, presents barriers to you ever reaching extraordinary.

★ Over to You

What story do you need to tell yourself to release your voice by just an extra 1°?

At an ACTION level, what will you do to tweak your voice so that your audience experiences something different? You could adapt: the pace, pitch, the tone, your pauses, your inflection, your energy, your rhythm or your choice of language. Give your voice some colour and a texture.

Choose a context to test this out. Just a small interaction you are due to have – five minutes only. Carve some words out so that the meaning and the emotion are aligned.

T-D-A.

Offering you the dare …

Jolt 10
Become the Chief of Possibility

Richard Branson thinks possibility. Benjamin Zander of the Boston Philharmonic Orchestra thinks possibility. Bradley Wiggins thinks possibility. James Dyson thinks possibility. Jeff Bezos, CEO of Amazon, thinks possibility. Richard Jordan from JPMorgan Chase also thinks possibility. Thinking with possibility opens up opportunities – it creates a platform for creativity and innovation. It leaves the door to your senses wide open to allow new ideas to enter.

Could I add your name to this list? Yes? No?

love my job title in BTFI. Fortunately, running my own business gives me permission to change my title everyday if I like. Lots of my clients tell me that they would love to have a job title like mine. Well, go on then. Do it. What are you waiting for? I know, I know, in your giant corporate organization where titles have to fit a formula and be approved by 199 different people from across the planet before getting sign off, it's almost impossible.

Do you really think you need to have your job title written in your email footer for it to be reality? My daughter has no email footer and that doesn't stop her being a global pop star, drama queen, Broadway actress, singer songwriter and occasionally a piano virtuoso. No, she uses her creativity to invent stuff in her head and off she goes …

> **'Creativity is just connecting things. When you ask creative people how they did something, they feel a little guilty because they didn't really do it, they just saw something.'**
>
> *Steve Jobs*

Do you currently spend your time being an architect of possibility or impossibility? Be honest. How much of your day do you spend looking to be creative, innovative, a rule breaker and an opportunity spotter?

Possibility Architects are not born. They are made over time and formed through constant practise of the right habits. Malcolm Gladwell, in his book *Outliers*, clearly shows us that the extraordinary abilities used to create and innovate possibility are not special powers reserved for the few. They are available to you too if you choose to practise the right THINKING and take the best course of ACTION.

> Possibility is an attitude. It will become your habit if you practise well.

What do those that THINK possibility actually do then? What differentiates them from the rest? I'm going to list those qualities and habits now for you. Before I do, I want to manage the fallout from those of you that know you have a tendency for *impossibility* and right now are a little grumpy with me. Looking at the *impossible* has its place if it is used appropriately. It can be grounding. It can plug us all back into reality. It offers a sense check. It can be the sign post that warns us all to pay attention to the right stuff at the right time. It can be a Jolt if you use it well. However, if it is your dominant THINKING style and habit, it will be a barrier to your ability to generate more extraordinary moments. In isolation, it will almost certainly trip you up.

By just 1°, here are some of the habits you will need to adopt to start THINKING with possibility.

Ask the right questions – Knowing that we will make this work, what do we need to do right now? There is a solution, how can we find it? If we were to remove all the difficulties and issues immediately, how would we proceed? Ask 'what if' more than 'why'. Start your questions with the word 'Imagine' or 'Supposing'.

By asking the right questions you create a new invention and shift the focus from *can't* to *can*. It tricks the mind. It may well jar, in an uncomfortable way for some, until it becomes seen as your new way to think. What other open questions could you ask?

Create the conditions that allow you to think – Life whizzes by. Your business decisions may need to be made rapidly. To start THINKING with possibility does require you to create the right conditions, the right time and the right space for people to entertain new ideas. Squeezing this into a 10-minute meeting and turning into another 'task to tick off the list' will not get you what you want. If you really want to build a space full of new ideas, make it important enough. Otherwise, don't bother.

Watch more porn – Nah, just kidding. However, you need to fuel your senses and get your idea juices gushing. You need to choose to disrupt your normal routine. You can do this in many ways: take a new route to work, read a paper that you would never choose, listen to a new artist on your iPod, watch a film from a different genre, talk to the person next to you in the queue (not in a stalker-ish kind of way!), eat something that you have never had before. You get my drift – shake up your normal! We can be creatures of habit – this will not breed possibility.

Remove your judgement hat – while encouraging those around you to take theirs off too. I frequently see the possibility for creative insights stopped very early on by someone hurling in a dose of judgement. Even if you are not immediately convinced by an idea, put your possibility hat on and ask the right questions. Stay curious. Demonstrate this through your tone of voice and the way you listen to the ideas of others. Constantly invite new THINKING, challenge and more 'what if' moments.

Wear other people's shoes – Not stealing them, just stepping into them. Research shows us that if we start to think about creating possibilities through the lens that others look through, it can open up new ideas. So, ask yourself, how would Apple tackle this issue? If Google were to be faced with this problem, what would they do next? If we all worked for Disney, how would we look at this differently?

Have a Doodle session – I once worked with a director that encouraged Doodle sessions. We didn't really have to doodle, although we could if we thought it would help. It was a set period of time, often no more than three to five minutes, where we needed to generate new ideas and start afresh. Anything goes. No limits. Blank sheet of paper time. Only once we had done this could we start to make connections and ask the 'What if' questions …

Adopting these habits will mean you begin to live out your new job title as Chief of Possibility. It needs some focus from you though. It does require you to carve out the time and space. No one will come to you tomorrow and give you additional time in your day to be more creative. You have to make it happen yourself.

I ran a workshop recently for a client that focused specifically on being a Possibility Architect. At the close of the day, one lady told me that she was astounded at what the group had achieved and created and that if you really give something your full attention and focus, without distractions, you could create amazing things. 'Yes', I said, 'correct'. Her response then surprised me, 'But it's not like that in my organization – it's full of distractions – so it's impossible to use anything from today!'

How fascinating. There she was, having had a live experience and a model of how extraordinary musicians create more possibility, yet she was not willing to take it on board. Of course it wasn't her current reality, which was why her organization was running the workshop in the first place. It was unhelpful to think that she would go back to her office and spend a day free from distractions becoming totally focused on being more creative. However, what would have been useful would be to take the learning and insight and apply it for 5 minutes during her day, 10 minutes at the most. Ten minutes to bundle up all of the THINKING and ACTION that she knew worked, test it out and then see what becomes possible. This is when the magic happens.

I am fairly confident that your work environment will also be full of distractions that hoover up your time. Therefore, how much of your day do you allow to be 'governed by the distractions' and how much of your day do you choose to own? Remember, all of these Jolts need only be adopted by 1°. The ripple effect will be significant.

★ Over to You

Imagine yourself as Chief of Possibility in your organization.

What would that mean you do differently right now?

Where have you got yourself stuck as Chief of Impossibility? Who around you is doing that job even better than you? Too much impossibility in your team and you're stuffed.

Which of these habits will you now adopt? And your first 1° step is....?

Take control. Do it. Be it. Now.

Jolt 11

Make your audience matter

The arts world presents us with a lens that demonstrates the importance of getting it right for your audience. No audience = no show. It's not complicated. With tens of millions of pounds being invested in a show, the stakes are high. Does that guarantee a success? Of course not. If it doesn't land for the audience, it hasn't worked. If you have the cash, time and resources to 'create theatre' for the sake of it and to massage your own artistic pleasure, lucky you. For most though, that is not the reality. Leading an organization places a responsibility on you to know your audience well, to know what they want and to be one step ahead in delivering that. Ignore them at your peril …

'The play was a great success, but the audience was a disaster.'

Oscar Wilde

I adore that quote. Just for a moment, it can ease the pain when your performance falls flat on its backside – oh the light relief that can come from blaming your audience …

Shockingly, I stumble across many leaders that take up residence in that thinking:

'If it hasn't worked, it's their fault for not getting it.'

'They said they wanted it like that, and that's what they got.'

'Tough! They're just a difficult customer.'

'Oh well. Most people liked it so that's not really my problem …'

'Who cares what they want?!'

I have heard all of those comments. Yes, honestly. When I heard the last one, I spluttered my coffee in a rather ungainly fashion all over the poor lady in front of me! The chap that made the comment, genuinely acted from that THINKING – 'Who cares what they want?!'

This Jolt is quite simple really: It's not about YOU; it's about your audience. This is another core practice of your journey towards extraordinary. A pre-requisite of adopting the Artful approach is to step into this Jolt. Failing to take this one on for yourself leaves you running the risk of being an orchestrator of the ordinary. And you don't want that, do you? Do you?!

For a cast of actors and singers, delivering eight shows a week in front of an audience always presented a clear indication to us of what was working and what wasn't. It was a moment by moment feedback loop. On the big shows, we were confident that we would have a full house for every performance. It was rarely a problem getting the bums on seats. In the long term of course, the measure of success was continuing to have full houses, night after night.

For you in your business, what is your longer term measure for success?

More customers?

Repeat customers?

Continued revenue?

World domination?

Acquisition?

A culture that people want to connect with?

…?

For you to achieve extraordinary things, using any one of those measures, means you must pay close attention: spot trends, listen, respond, think ahead, look around you …

> You have to get yourself hot, steamy and all turned on to notice the choices you have.

You know that though don't you? We will talk about that more later on in the book. Although, despite my asking you a question that I assume you would say yes to, I have been introduced to new clients over the years that have wanted to be successful, have used more than one of the measures above and yet still haven't delivered what their audience wanted.

Why was that?

Well, one reason was that they had become so immersed in what they were delivering and stuck in their own heads that they failed to spot the many choice points that they had where there was the possibility to add even more value to their audience. They had become consumed with their own greatness: 'We're marvellous, we have fabulous clients, we get good feedback …' They would keep running this loop and didn't spot soon enough that listening to any internal chatter on *repeat*, means taking up residence inside your own head and not being where the action is.

Whether you run your own empire or help someone else to run theirs, you do need clarity on your long-term measure of success. It might be one from the list above, and the likelihood is that you will have your own specific measurable.

Perhaps the greater challenge is not for those that sit at the top of their organizations, but for those that need to translate the vision and make it real across the rest of the organization. Many of my clients tell me, on a regular basis, that people across their business are far too disconnected from their audience. They are busy being busy: churning out widgets because that's what their job description says, yet having little understanding of whether what they do each day touches the audience and hits the success measure button.

Theatre is intimate. You know whether the audience is with you. You need only look and listen to get the insight. For big organizations it is not always as straightforward as that, as you may be working within multiple levels of hierarchy and therefore further away from seeing what really lands.

So, what is the solution for you?

As a leader, start the conversation. Yep, that's the beginning point. How often do you have a dialogue with your team that Jolts them into considering your audience? I see some of my client teams do this on a daily basis. I see many that never have the conversation.

Why is that?

Because they don't care enough, because it isn't relevant to them, because they are too busy, because it's not their job, because they don't really know who their audience is …?

Well, what questions do you need to be asking?

Who is your audience?

Don't be fooled into thinking that 'audience' simply means your customers. Your audience is the people that you need to connect and engage with to make stuff happen. In your working day, your audience will constantly shift: the sales team, marketing, your CEO, the board, suppliers, your team, your family, the people that run your reception desk … it's an endless list. This is why the questions have to become a habit. You cannot just ask them once a year at a team off-site!

What is important to them?

Take a moment to step into the world of your audience: what do they expect from you? What matters to them most? What have they told you in the past about what works and what doesn't work for them?

Have you acted on that? What is *their* measure of success? What does extraordinary look like for them?

How do you know you are delivering?

What signs are you looking for to see if your audience is happy, connected, excited, inspired, moved …? Are you out there listening and looking? Are you present and reacting to what you notice?

So, are YOU having the conversation?

Are you asking these questions of yourself and your team?

If you are asking the right questions, are you asking them regularly enough?

If you aren't having these conversations, it can only mean one thing – your focus is locked deeply inside your head, the heads of your team and the micro world that you have created around you. It's easily done, I recognize that. And as much as that might be a place of huge comfort for you, it will not be your winning ticket to extraordinary. It just can't be.

As we discussed right up front, the world is moving at a frightening pace. No organization, team or leader can rely on just churning out the same old stuff day in, day out. As audience members ourselves, our choices over where we buy from are expanding daily and most of us will take advantage of that by shopping around. The internet has created a massive explosion of choice and we don't have to do much digging around before we find alternatives; some better, some worse.

I am under no illusion whatsoever that my customers can, at any minute, up sticks and find a coach, consultant or speaker that is more extraordinary than me. There are lots out there. If I become complacent and spend too much time thinking about me, without focusing on my audience, it won't be long before the audience is gone …

It IS all about your audience. You will soon discover that the moment you start to THINK this and take the relevant ACTION, you will begin the transformation process.

★ Over to You

How will you adopt this Jolt as your new habit?

Take some time to ask yourself the questions I posed. Carve out some time with your team and have the conversation with them too.

How will you adapt your THINKING and your ACTION by just 1°, now?

Making this a habit requires repetition. Include those questions in every team meeting. Graffiti the walls with them. Tattoo them across your forehead. Have novelty mugs made emblazoned with 'It's not about you, it's about your audience'.

The sooner you and your team realize the importance of an audience focus, the sooner you will soar …

Dizzy heights await …

Jolt 12
Change the language to change the story

Hopefully, you may find that by perhaps trying out these jolts you could discover some benefit; but there's no guarantee of course. It might happen though. If you try enough that is. I mean, don't worry about not getting it all right. But maybe if you don't panic, you will possibly discover that you might just not have to put up with ordinary after all. Well. Maybe. You can at least try. But don't give up hope if you don't succeed …

Oh, the pain that it gave me to write that. However, I imagine it's nothing compared to the pain you endured from reading it. For some audiences though, that is their normal experience from the people who want to connect with them, or *try* to! They do so in exactly that way. Yikes. It drives me to the edge of insanity.

'Do or do not … there is NO try.'

Yoda, Star Wars.

I am often accused of catching flies, as apparently my jaw drops that far when I am aghast at some of the things I see and hear in organizations. These are real people, running big organizations, often paid in gold bars, with giant responsibilities, a vast audience to seduce and a need to ignite some passion. So, with all that in mind, you might think that their messages and dialogue would have a bit of razzle dazzle, right? Some oomph? Some precision? Messages that connect and sparkle?! Create a sense of theatre and wonder?! Call people to action …?!

Occasionally, yes. Most often, no!

I want to get into the meaty part of this Jolt so I won't dribble on with theatrical tales of linguistic mastery! Suffice to say though, I have crossed paths with numerous mammoth brained, Artful folks: intelligent, well read and switched on, that have their many qualifications tattooed across their foreheads. However, they have been unable to connect with people at any level. Their choice of words and use of restrictive language has left their audience baffled and disengaged.

Study hard. Learn lots. Be a master of your niche. Know more than others.

These are all extremely important to nail.

And … more important than all of them, weave in language that connects your messages and seduces your audience.

The first paragraph of this Jolt illustrated a handful of the trap doors that people fall through. It's so very painful when they are all shoved together in that way. Master the alternatives and you will transform the way you unite with your audience.

I popped it all in a table below as I think this will be the easiest way for you grasp it quickly.

Beware of the trap door …	Masterful language …
'We will **try** and get that done in time.' The word try implies impossibility. If you use it, you have given yourself permission to fail. I see people 'trying to sing' – they give a half-hearted attempt that is neither good or rubbish. They claim to have tried …	'We **will** get that done in time.' Be definite. Fully commit to doing the thing in front of you. Be accountable. Use words that show your commitment. No use building in wiggle room – just say 'I will …'

(continued)

Beware of the trap door ...	Masterful language ...
'**Don't** worry about not being confident enough ...'	'**Stay calm and focused** and you will feel more confident.'
To give the command of 'Don't worry' requires me to worry and then stop worrying! It's the only way our brains can process a don't. Notice how often you give commands to yourself and others of all the things you don't want.	Give instructions based on the state and action that you DO want: Stay calm, relax now, be your best, be confident, walk slowly ...
'**Maybe** give it a go and you might **possibly** discover a better way ...'	'**Do it**, see what happens and you will learn loads ...!'
These are buffer words and also imply impossibility. They will set doubt in the minds of your audience.	Lose the buffer words. They serve no purpose. Be clear, concise and sure. If your language is scattered with them, check in with your THINKING.
'I hear what you are saying. You make a good point ... **BUT**... I don't think it will work.'	'I hear what you are saying. You make a good point **and** I think we need to talk about the best way to do this ...'
But negates what has gone before it. It draws our focus to the second part of the statement only. This one trips many people up.	Use co-joined **and** to link statements. This will revolutionize the way your messages are received.
'I know that I **should** go and see him...'	'I **will** go and see him' or 'I **won't** go and see him.'
Should is often someone else's rule or a rule of your own that is out of date. When you hear it, ask the question, 'Should? According to whom?'	Once you have asked that question, then decide if it is something you want to do or don't want to do. Then make the most adult choice.

Some of you will think that what I'm blabbering on about is pure semantics. Go and put it into practice and I am confident that once you have tested these out will you see how powerful a response you can elicit with such tiny tweaks to your language. I get a whole heap of emails each day from clients that learnt about this on one of our workshops, each one describing the significant shift in relationships they found just based on using transformational language. It's small stuff that creates big stuff. Honest.

> Language shapes our culture and tells the story. Change your language and you change the story.

I am sure you will have your own view on why so much of our conversation and language has become littered with these words that 'pad out', create a buffer and distract from the intended message. So, what is it? Laziness, habit, cultural norms? It is probably, to some degree, all of these. I also think that people have become much less confident in committing to their message and being held accountable for the output. It seems as though for many of us, we find ourselves operating in a climate of fear where the price for over-committing or making a mistake can seem huge. Taking a straight-talking message, owning it and delivering it, requires a shot of bravery.

Our words are not just plucked out of thin air. We choose them, albeit at times unconsciously, based on our experiences. This brings me back to the challenge I have offered you throughout the book: the more time you spend with your radar turned up high, in the moment, looking and listening, the more space you will gain to make better choices. It will allow you to craft the words you use and make the relevant upgrade as opposed to just running tired old habits. Extraordinary moments and extraordinary experiences will be built.

Each one of the masterful language examples that I gave you has the power to shape an enabling or disabling mindset. It's amazing how one misplaced word can make the difference between your success or failure.

★ **Over to You**

Start by running a little experiment. Spend 10 minutes noticing the language that you and those around you use. I bet you will be surprised at the number of Trap Doors that are created just from those small words.

The written effect of these words is potent too. Notice how emails become scattered with them.

Which ones trip you up most? Be honest with yourself.

Now, what are you committing to do to change this? Tell your team, family and other colleagues the mission you are on. Get them on board. This will go viral.

Do it. Make it happen. Be bold. Choose. Watch. See what bounces back.

Listen to Yoda ...

Jolt 13
Get yourself all turned on ...

We are living in a technological age where our attention and focus is pulled all over the place. It is becoming increasingly hard to engage with the present. In order that you make the best choices and decisions on anything in life, you have to be here: right now, in this moment and very turned on. Having more extraordinary moments in your life requires you to spend more time in this moment. Not the moment that has just passed. Not the one that hasn't yet arrived. But this one, right now. The greatest artists and the greatest leaders become so by spending most time in the present, forming a decision and then taking action.

> **Manawa** – Now is the moment of power.

That's a powerful statement isn't it? Manawa – the only moment where we have real power and influence is right here, right now. The moment that has just passed us by has gone … the moment that is peeking at us from around the corner is not yet here. THIS is the moment where we hold greatest power so why on earth would you lose that moment by being anywhere other than here?!

Manawa is one of the Hawaiian Huna principles – a philosophy that comes from over 100 years of tradition and rules for living a rounded life. It feels like a relevant way to capture the essence of this Jolt.

This Jolt is a biggie. It will be an uncomfortable wallop if you take the hit and it will form a major part of your transformation.

As I alluded to at the start of the book, I am a big Apple fan. I love my iPhone, iPad and Macbook. However, there is a fine line between my deep love for the benefits they offer my life and the hatred I have for them and the way I allow them to suck my attention away from the here and now. I know I'm not alone with this. I look around board rooms, conference suites, coffee shops, theatres and trains with the same story being played out: people allowing themselves to be dragged away from this moment and into some techno parallel universe.

Consider for a moment just how much time you spend being really present and fully turned on during the day.

If you were to wave a wand and spend just five minutes in your day being completely immersed in the moment and fully aware, which five minutes would you choose?

To clarify, before some of you start getting hot under the collar, by fully turned on I mean with your radar fully turned on. I know what you were thinking …

I want to tell you about my very good friend and BTFI team player, Al Gurr. I have not changed his name for the purpose of confidentiality, as I want you to know all about him! He is awesome. Al is a master of many things. It is not simply his persistence and tenacity that makes him so extraordinary but his ability to be in the moment with his radar switched on and absorbing his surroundings. Much of Al's time in life is spent playing extraordinary jazz in his role as a musician. However, his ability to spot an opportunity to transform something from ordinary to extraordinary is second to none. For Al, spotting the opportunity alone is not enough. Once he has spotted it, he will take some ACTION to see what's possible as he knows that this is what will ultimately transform the performance. Al does this. Consistently.

Is he a creative soul? Oh yes. Does he search out new upgrades? Of course. Does he strive for extraordinary? Absolutely. Does he screw things up? Lots! Does he have some super special power only available to him? Yes. Actually no, of course he doesn't.

What Al does, is to stay turned on. His radar is working overtime. On some of our team workshops, Al plays the piano and accompanies the singers. Observing his mastery teaches not only the group but me too, loads. Because he is in the room, alert, watching, listening and reacting to what he sees, this enables him to spot the moments where something can improve. He can see the potential to upgrade. Once he's spotted something, he will ask the question. Of course it's not always about making the upgrade. Being able to spot when something is working brilliantly and then to offer that insight is key too.

> When you are on the stage, BE on the stage.

Whilst rehearsing my final production at Music College, I found myself standing on stage with another member of the company. It was not 'my moment' in the scene and the focus was very much elsewhere on stage. At the time I took that as a cue to chitter chatter about my plans for the evening ahead. Surely that's ok? It wasn't my scene so who would be watching me …? Was I present, with my radar on …? Errr, no.

Out of nowhere, booming over the auditorium sound system comes 'Richard … when you are on the stage, **be** on the stage. Thank you!'

Yikes. Jolt! So someone was watching me?!

I had managed to fool myself into thinking that I could get away with being on the stage but not actually *being* there. That message hit home.

So where's your stage? The office, the theatre, the boardroom, the kitchen, the sports field? So when you are on your stage, are you **really** on it? Are you actually there in body and in mind? On a scale of 0–10, how high is your radar turned up?

What I see the majority of the time in organizations, is that people are physically on the stage but with their mind elsewhere and their radar pointed inwards. This not only limits choice, it removes all possibility to be extraordinary. Wherever you are, be fully there.

> Be in the room: alert, watching, listening, noticing, choosing and reacting.

So, is being present easy then? Ha, hell no. Being present and in this moment asks you to quieten down your inner chatter and, for that moment, to park your inner critic. Unless you have some special, inborn power that enables you to flick the switch on or off, it will undoubtedly require that you practise, practise, practise. It's one of those things that need you to be able to trust that you have the right SKILLS and ACTION in place to do the thing in front of you.

★ Over to You

As I have already said, being present, in this moment and **on** the stage will require you to practise.

For the next seven days, I want you to choose one thing, each day, where you commit to whack your radar up to 10. It might just be for two minutes. Believe me, even two minutes will be a big success. Choose something different each day.

Remember: having your radar on means pointing your awareness out of your own head.

As soon as you realize that your attention has slipped back inside yourself and inner chatter has started, simply acknowledge that and get back in the moment.

Being in the moment will bring you many new opportunities. Go on: grab them.

Jolt 14
Fly by the seat of your pants

In such a rapid-fire world where both opportunities and challenges are flying towards you in equal measure, agile thinking and nimble footwork will be a key factor in successfully navigating them. The only thing you can be sure of in the work place of the future is that it is set to get busier and more complex. Your audience expectation will increase and the speed of delivery and response will need an almighty Jolt. For you and your team to flourish, knowing when to take action and then taking it will enable you to stay one step ahead …

A major part of the excitement and attraction of live theatre is the unpredictability. Despite there being a script to follow, a musical score to work with and a stage management team to bring the action together, there will always remain that sense of 'anything can happen at any moment' which is not the case in some other art forms. I dabbled with a bit of TV in my time – not watching it I might add, but being on it. I did a couple of commercials and although I enjoyed the difference and variety from the 'eight shows a week' lifestyle, I didn't quite discover the same thrill that comes from doing live theatre in front of a live audience. Or even live theatre in front of a dead audience …

> Live theatre forces the performers to remain on their toes, making quick decisions when required. Extraordinary Leadership requires you to do the same.

I could write an entire book on all the things that happened whilst I was on stage that jolted me to make a quick decision about what to do next: no wig mistress in the wings, so no wig – just a stocking cap on my head, no trousers to go with my costume on a quick change, no leading lady on stage with me during a love scene, no lights, no music and once, no recollection of why I was even standing on a stage with 3000 people staring at me. Sadly that resulted in no recollection of the lyrics to my song and therefore about 20 seconds of 'shmana hana hah-ing'. I even had friends watching the show that night and, do you know what, they didn't even notice! On reflection, I can view each of those moments with great fondness and laughter … now. At the time I'm not so sure that was my reaction.

My point is this – s**t happens – you can't avoid it. That's the nature of flying by the seat of your pants to create something extraordinary for your audience.

Remember: It's not what happens TO you, it's what you CHOOSE to do about it …

In your organization, regardless of what your business offers, you are putting on a piece of live theatre everyday: seducing your audience, communicating messages, changing lives, challenging people's thinking, offering something new to buy, helping people feel better about themselves or engaging people in a new story. Even with the best script in place, the best cast and the best theatre, if you are really chasing a performance that is extraordinary, you will also face that unpredictability every day.

Right, take a moment now to step into the notion that you are creating live theatre each day. As you do so, consider how equipped you and your team are to deal with that degree of unpredictability? If you were to go on stage with no trousers, what on earth would you do and how would you put a solution in place?

For all the Jolts I'm offering you, their success lies in you grabbing them by the balls and practising them. You will not get them by osmosis. Simply reading this book will not make you extraordinary. Sorry for any disappointment caused by that fact. Actually, I'm not sorry at all! Get up off your backside and take action – and only then will you dabble with extraordinary.

Ok, so here is a way to navigate the unpredictable nature of live theatre, leadership and more generally, being a human being!

I learnt this when I trained as a Cognitive Behavioural Hypnotherapist. Even all the mixed up folks I worked with when I ran a therapy clinic found great benefit in this framework. You don't need to be in a trance for it to work either …

It's as simple as A, B and C …

So, pretend that you've spotted in an instant that you need to tackle what is in front of you differently. Here goes:

A for Affect – decide how you want to *affect* the situation you find yourself in: how do you want it to be different? How do you want it to change course? What are *you* going to do to *affect* that change? This is a bit like setting an outcome, although there is rarely the time to plod through an eight-step process when you need to make a decision in the moment.

B for Behaviour – what do you actually need to do now to make this happen? How do you need to behave? KISS – Keep it so simple! This might be about what you say, how you say it, how you stand, how you walk, who you talk to and where you place your eye line. Decide on the practical ACTION you are going to take.

C for Cognition – a poncy word for thinking! What do you need to THINK now that will drive your behaviour and then affect the situation in the way that you want? As we have established throughout the book, pointing your mind in the right direction is a critical step in taking on an Artful approach.

> A … B … C … then do it!

I was always amazed at how rapidly my clients that came to me for therapeutic support took this approach on, and made it a part of their unconscious competence. A, B, C will soon become your habit too.

★ Over to You

So, only dare to go on stage without your trousers if you are taking part in The Full Monty … otherwise, keep them on.

A, B, C is a really sexy framework to use to Jolt your own thinking.

To help you get it in the muscle, carve out some opportunities where you can practise this.

Even sitting in a meeting, before you contribute and make your point, do A, B, C.

However you choose to make it your new habit, just make it your new habit. No faffing. Get active.

Jolt 15
Live out the Magic 'If'...

A culture is built upon beliefs, values, an identity, rituals, stories and traditions. As humans, we are made up of the same. They become the basis of the many extraordinary moments that we create in life. If we are not careful though, they can also form the basis of the many limitations we place on others and ourselves. In one moment they are a part of our brilliance and in the next we are tripping over them. Oh to be able to see them differently and then change them ...

As you know, my work as a coach and speaker is to bring these Jolts into organizations, to enable them to absorb the thinking and start acting out a new story. I am not interested in the fluffy bolt-on behaviours. When faced with the choice to tackle the cause or the effect, I will challenge and unpick the cause every time. Why fiddle with the effect only? At some point, the cause will just find a new way to bite your arse. Be brave and tackle the real issues, I say. It is worth reminding you again that every choice in life comes with a consequence though – it may not be something catastrophic but there will be consequences all the same. Sometimes it will be something as small as extra energy you need to spend, more time needed or a dose of fresh discomfort. And you know how much I like that!

> Every choice you make will come with consequences. That includes your choice to do nothing!

A few years ago I was asked to work with a senior partner at an International law firm. Her name was Georgina. The head of L&D brought me in as she believed my 'face it out' approach could be the way to unlock her 'stuckness and resistance' perceived by the majority of the organization. She had built a strong reputation on being someone that lived by the principle of 'the world according Georgina' is the only way to go.

You may know some people like that. They might not be called Georgina though. They come with various names and in all shapes and sizes. Perhaps you occasionally step into 'the world according to me' attitude … just a thought …

Anyway, I met with Georgina and she proceeded to spend the first 20 minutes walloping me: giving me her views on coaching, development, the organization, my credentials, my theatrical past and how there was little chance of me being able to help her. Oh joy! I am flooded with a giant surge of excitement when a session kicks off in this way.

Eventually I got myself on her radar with some tough prodding and poking. It seemed that being provocative, by 1° more than she was, ensured she stopped talking and started listening. I am not a believer in long-winded, month-on-month coaching sessions. I expect a lot from my clients and they, in turn, should expect a great deal from me. With that in mind, I tend to work at a pace. This session was no different. I was going for 'cause' over 'effect' as there was no point in dressing up the issues with just some fluffy new behaviours. They are rarely sustainable.

Re-visit the Performance model from earlier in the book. Making a real difference with Georgina was going to require her to make some adaptations at the THINK and IDENTITY level. Changes at these levels would open up choices. This in turn would unlock the doorway to some new ACTION.

I decided to offer Georgina the option of having a mirror held up to her. She was intrigued – and this was seemingly driven by the idea that I couldn't possibly have anything to tell her that would make an ounce of difference and that she hadn't heard before! Having spent an hour with her already, and based on her impact on me, I had lots to share with her. As I do, I told it as I saw it.

This was seemingly the game-changer. Our conversation freed up. Why? Because no one had ever bothered to take the time to share anything like this with her – what she had heard, for over 20 years, was a monotone moaning and complaining about her faults. Let's be clear, I am sure some people in that time had attempted to deliver some feedback that was more useful, but it was already too late. Georgina had decided that all feedback was criticism, personally aimed at attacking her and taking her down. She had closed off a long time ago.

So, what happened next? We started to unpick some of Georgina's THINKING. What struck us both was how out of date it was. She had a hard drive and software that was still operating on the Sinclair platform, whilst those around her had upgraded to Apple Yosemite! This was causing major issues and had done over a long period of time.

Even Georgina herself recognized that some key pieces of her THINKING were stuck and no longer did the job that she had originally intended.

The question she asked next, though, was one that many people grapple with …

'How do I upgrade my THINKING when I've mastered so much that is unhelpful? How can I change a belief to something more useful?'

Stanislavski, the pioneer of method acting, had a solution for that very question, as every actor he worked with wrestled with the same challenge: 'How can I live out a belief, an identity and a story that is not *currently* my reality and that I have not experienced before?'

Stanislavski is the father of modern theatre technique and his formula for creating authentic performance is still taught today in every theatre school around the world. He spotted a problem when working with young actors: how could they possibly adopt a character without having previously experienced *their* emotions and *their* experiences? It was here that he devised the notion of the *Magic If* …

The question that Stanislavski challenged his actors to ask themselves was this:

What would I be doing now *if* I were living out this reality? *If* this were my story, how would I be THINKING and ACTING?

This question invited the actor to presuppose a new truth and to 'act as if' it were real. They may not have ever lived that experience before, but his question opened up their imagination to start pretending. Our brains' capacity to imagine and to then turn that imagination into experience is incredible. Stanislavski knew that and made a point of helping the actors stretch their own thinking and possibility.

During the sessions with Georgina, we flipped between recognizing what was in the mirror, what she wanted to adapt now and what she needed to act as *if* it were true for her to move forward. It was a 1° process. She made the tiniest of tweaks. The most significant being a move from 'Feedback is only given to make me look stupid so therefore just ignore it' to her *Magic If* story of 'Feedback offers me new choices and choice is good'. This was immensely freeing for her and meant that instead of fighting with her colleagues, she started to welcome their views, in the knowledge that it presented more choices than she had before. I still see Georgina every now and then. It is work in progress and some days she still needs to give herself a bigger Jolt to step deeper into her Magic If …

And the audience perception at performance review time? She's transformed.

Actor, leader, entrepreneur, parent, president – whatever you are and whatever you want to become, the Magic If opens up the possibility for you to get closer to it and better at it. It gives the new story some air time and, in a very simple way, encourages you to play with it. What makes it all the more robust is that it is not focused on changing your past story but looks to build the new one that will take you forward.

★ Over to You

When do you want to start telling yourself and your audience a new story?

What THINKING upgrade are you finding hard to budge?

Decide on the story, decide what you want and decide what new THINKING needs to be installed.

So, ask yourself this:

What would I be doing now *if* I were living out this reality? *If* this were my story, how would I be THINKING and ACTING?

Scribble down your thoughts ...

And the first action step you are going to take now is ...?

Jolt 16
Stay plugged in

There is nothing quite like it: watching the most elegant and connected company of dancers do their thing, as one. Seeing how the focus of the performance becomes so interchangeable is mesmerizing – your eye can take you anywhere on the stage and you are sure to see a part of the story being played out. This is an extraordinary team dynamic. If you gaze into the sporting world or on any high performing team you will see the same; connection, accountability and communication. Now imagine transporting that same approach into a team in your organization – this is where the magic begins and the transformation takes place.

spend numerous hours each week observing teams and their interplay. I have my work hat on with my clients and I have my Artful hat on when I go to see theatre or music. I get excited easily. I know, weird. I find it fascinating though. The dynamics of what I see – the spoken and the unspoken, seduce me. Some of it is subtle and some of it is bold. Characters will float to the top and others will disappear to the bottom … occasionally never to return.

A few months ago, a very good friend of mine offered me tickets to see his daughter in a production that was visiting London for the first time. They are an American dance company called Pilobulus. If you get a chance to catch them somewhere, go. Cancel everything else in your diary and make sure you are there. They are breathtaking. If you cannot buy a ticket, steal one!

The production they brought over was called Shadowlands. The concept is simple; a small company of dancers that tell a story using minimal props but heavily reliant upon lighting and shadow to create the effects and bring the story to life. The cast are in full view for most of the performance – they control and move the lights on stage, they move the scenery, they change costumes and act entirely as one.

What struck me most though was this – as I looked around the stage, at every single moment each one of them was totally absorbed in the overall story they needed to tell. Even with one solo dancer taking centre stage, everyone else continued to perform their own part and remained a contribution. Extraordinary. It is a physically and mentally gruelling piece of theatre. The demands put upon them are quite incredible. For me, this made it even more amazing that they each stayed plugged in throughout, despite it not being their solo moment.

The call to action here, for you, is this: it may not be your moment on stage, you may not be the focus point but **you are still performing**.

It's not rocket science is it?

The Pilobulus dance company are not just extraordinary dancers (although each one of them is certainly a master of their art). It is not that they just have a brilliant story to work with or an audience that give them lots of love. It isn't just that they woo the audience with feats of physical prowess that elevate what they do to extraordinary. All of those components matter. They really do. The element that binds it all together is their THINKING – the Artful attitude at play that means, throughout the performance, they are *each* performing at *every* moment.

How true is that attitude for you?

How visible is that trait within your team?

How much is it encouraged across your culture?

I think it is rare to see this played out in organizations. So much of the story being told each day has become transactional – it is one task passed from you to the next person. The baton is handed over at such speed. While you have the baton, it is your moment. Once the baton has been passed on, your moment has ended and the performance ends.

Your business world will undoubtedly be becoming more virtual based: conference calls, tele-presence sessions, webinars. If it isn't already, it is going to go that way in time. Seemingly though, this is making it even harder for people to stay connected and to keep the performance running. I often sit as a part of conference calls with my clients. Much of what I see is quite surprising. I observe leaders that step up to the mark, deliver their messages well and in an engaging manner and then, as soon as they are done, they switch off, become distracted and get lost in their stuff.

I recently challenged a senior leader that I coach on this. I observed it playing out during a global conference call where he was responsible for delivering some big messages. What this required, though, was not simply the transaction of handing the messages over. No, it needed him to remain *in the performance*. Only by doing so would he be able to make sense of people's reactions, their concerns and their excitement. Just because his moment had passed, did not mean the show was over.

The problem with leaving this as it is and making it ok, is that you end up performing an organizational show that is disparate and disconnected.

Look, I'm not saying that you shouldn't carve out some downtime during your day where it is ok to be lost in your own head. It's a natural human response to get distracted and to divert your attention away from the action. What I want you to consider is this:

Has delivering your part of the action and then switching off the performance become your norm and your current habit?

This Jolt is designed to put the choice back on your radar.

Return to the Performance Map for a moment – what level is currently the blocker that stops you spending more time performing?

> SPACE – you will do it *here* but not *there?* (go to THINK and ask yourself how come?)

> ACTION? – you don't know *what* to do?

SKILLS – you don't know *how* to do it?

THINK – you *can't*, you don't *want* to, it's just *not important* enough ...?

IDENTITY – perhaps it's just not *who* you are ...

Which level do you need to nudge then? As always, be honest with yourself.

Whether you keep your performance switched on or not, your audience will still have a perception of you. Your brand will continue to play out and be seen.

Dan Goleman, writer and researcher on emotional intelligence, conducted an experiment at Harvard University many years ago about the optimum time we all have to make an impact on people. The number is widely known and I guess you will have heard it before.

Thirty seconds. The first 30 seconds is the amount of time we have to get our brand out there and stored in the mind of our audience. On the back of this, Goleman asked the question: 'as the audience, what do we do with the data that we get from someone in the first 30 seconds of meeting them?'

The answer? We gauge the person's competency within 80% accuracy! It makes me shudder every time I share that – so, based on the way I dress, my language, my eye contact, the way I sit, stand, walk, someone will judge how competent I am as a coach, speaker, parent, friend, human being ...

The message in here is simple.

1. Make sure you are putting the right messages out there when you perform. Does your brand land? Would your audience take away the experience of you that you *want* them to have?

2. People will have a view of you whatever you are doing. When you are 'singing' – out there strutting your stuff as a leader – in those moments where you switch the performance off, people will still have a view. They will still make a judgement. You are still seen.
3. Extraordinary teams are created when people continue to perform, even when it is not their solo moment. Go and watch Pilobulus or any team that thinks in this way and you will instantly know what I mean.

Your brand continues to play out long after that first 30 seconds. In the many moments during your day that you may not be singing, *remember that you* **are** *still performing.*

★ Over to You

Here's a starting point for the action you can take:

During your day, the performance your organization gives cannot switch off.

Choose a scenario from your day where you may not be singing and yet you know you need to stay switched on and performing.

Which level do you need to tinker with to make the shift; some new THINKING to drive new ACTION?

Go small. Go for the touch point that will add greater value to the overall outcome

And your 0–10 on your scale of commitment is … ?!

Perhaps call on some Magic to help you …

Jolt 17
Embrace the art of being vulnerable

One myth that is frequently played out within organizations is that vulnerability is a sign of weakness. However, in the numerous conversations I have with my clients where they describe their moments of vulnerability, it is most often displayed when they are owning up to mistakes they made, finding the courage to set up their own business, driving forward major change agendas and taking their company public. None of these show weakness. In fact they demonstrate the complete opposite. Perhaps this then tells us that vulnerability is a strong measure of our courage. Showing vulnerability therefore needs to sit at the heart of your adventure towards extraordinary.

This is by far the toughest Jolt for me to write about and to then share with you. Why is that? Because for a long time I was deeply immersed in a fairly destructive cycle of perfectionism – my eternal quest for EVERYTHING to be just right – no flaws, no cock-ups, no looking silly: no vulnerability. Throughout this book I have been comfortable to reveal me: being honest and open with all that I share and yet I know that when I talk about me and vulnerability, it is the ultimate stretch …

In so many ways, my striving for perfection made up many of my moments of brilliance and yet, surprisingly, a second later, it would be the very same thing that tripped me up. Would I re-write that phase in my history though? No. Did I learn from it, YES! Do I now seek out the occasions to be exposed and more open? Yes, I have to. Do the moments of perfection still creep up on me when I least expect it? Oh yes, for sure. Frequently. Richard Tyler is work in progress!

When I think of my role models around me as I grew up, they didn't display vulnerability. I never had the chance to ask them the questions that would have shed more light on this. I can only assume that at a THINKING level, it was considered not the right thing to do: keep your emotions close, don't show your faults and don't let weakness be displayed for all to see.

It is rare that the words vulnerable and leadership appear in the same sentence. However, I believe that over the last 20 years society has become more open and accepting of the idea that vulnerability is a strength to be harnessed as opposed to a weakness that should be covered up.

'Vulnerability is about showing up and being seen. It's tough to do that when we're terrified about what people might see or think.'

Brene Brown

Many of the leaders that I coach stress their desire to be strong, qualified, smart, powerful, infallible and perfect. Very rarely do I meet a leader who focuses on the need to be honest and transparent – yet both of these qualities open you up and display a degree of vulnerability.

What qualities do you focus on as a leader? List them ...

Where does honesty and transparency feature in there? Or doesn't it?

What masks have you started wearing that have become your shield against showing vulnerability?

What do you think would be the effect of displaying greater transparency in your role? What is the risk?

I recognize that you may well display these traits within your own team. What happens though when you need to influence up the organization? How comfortable are you to display them then?

There is probably little value in attempting to unpick where you learnt to THINK and ACT as you currently do. The more useful thing to consider is what needs to be different for you moving ahead.

Despite my spending some time getting locked into an unhealthy perfection cycle, I felt as though I had a thorough insight into not only the strategy for exposing vulnerability but, as a performer, the purpose of it. Vulnerability presented me with the opportunity to be real. Being real was authentic. Being authentic opened up the channel to connect, engage and ultimately touch my audience. And, as you know, it's all about your audience.

'You will become way less concerned with what other people think of you when you realize how seldom they do ...'

David Foster Wallace

The vulnerability that a performer shares need be no different to the vulnerability that you as a leader also share. Here are some things for you to consider when taking on this Jolt:

1. Showing vulnerability requires great courage. It starts at THINK. What permission do you need to give yourself?
2. What would happen if you were to take on the outcome of being 'perfectly imperfect'? Strive for mistakes. Own the mishaps. That is all a part of being on the perfectly imperfect journey.
3. What do you do when you make a mistake? Own them – vulnerability requires you to admit the times when you screw up – not blame, not justify, not point fingers, not 'that is just who I am ...!' – be accountable. This builds your credibility. This will harness immense trust from those around you and signal to them that vulnerability relies on courage, not fear.
4. Share your fears, worries and concerns. This is not the same as 'being a victim'. Encourage yourself to be adult in the way that you share what troubles you. Admitting your fears will free you up and can have the effect of the fear itself dissolving. It will also give permission for

your team to be honest and share their fears and concerns too. Do not confuse this with 'dumping' your issues on others. This is about putting them out there and opening up the possibility for solutions to appear.

5. Ask for help. Sometimes this can be hard can't it? Being comfortable enough with yourself to admit that you don't have all the answers, can't do something or perhaps just want help making something happen, shows great strength. It may feel odd at first. It will soon become a habit that goes viral.

6. Take what you do seriously – give a s**t. Perhaps you don't need to take yourself quite so seriously though? Be prepared to laugh at yourself a bit more. Start to craft a culture where others have the freedom to do the same.

All of these need only be fiddled with by one 1°. This will get you moving. People will be a little surprised if you suddenly flick the vulnerability switch from off to on! This is not digital – it is analogue and therefore you need to turn the dial up and down as necessary.

Masks become a terrible distraction. The first time you slipped one on, you will have done it for all the right reasons to manage an uncomfortable situation that you faced – it will have helped you manage your reaction. The problems arise when the mask is left on and then another one is placed on top ... and another ... and so on. Even getting in the room with so many masks strapped to your face eventually becomes a challenge!!

For all the highly skilled and talented performers that are out there working, those that elevate themselves to extraordinary are those that dare themselves to open up. As a leader, if you are genuinely compelled to shake up your THINKING and ACTION, then you will also need to embrace the art of being vulnerable.

★ Over to You

What masks do you think you wear? What masks do your audience see you wearing?

On a scale of 0–10, how committed are you to removing them?

Practise leaving your ego at the door – what would that take?

In some contexts, with some people, you will show vulnerability – so what is it that makes that ok?

Unlike my usual wallop of 'get out there and be it', I want you to pay attention here and tread with greater care. Small and consistent steps will serve you better …

T-D-A springs to mind.

THINK – DECIDE – ACT

Jolt 18
Bring out the best version of yourself

We can all have bad days. Stuff happens. Sometimes it can just take moaning children, heavy traffic or that first meeting of the day with that really annoying idiot from the sales team to set your mood into decline, right? After that, it's a rollercoaster that mostly takes a nosedive, with a few twists and turns along the way. But what exactly will you do to disrupt your mood? For the people that get to spend time with you at the end of the day, there is little hope of survival! They will have you at your worst. The possibility of you in that state being able to unwrap any extraordinary moments has closed down. Another day gone and more opportunities lost. If it wasn't for the kids, the traffic and that bloke in sales this morning, it could have been oh so different …

S ound familiar? Each day, in any one moment, in businesses around the globe, you can guarantee that there will be leaders that run their day like this. Notice my use of language – 'run their day' – it is, after all, a choice they make. The day does not run you!

In the UK, before being given a licence to drive a car, you must display L-plates – this is to show (warn!) other motorists that you are a learner driver and that mistakes are likely. I am only bothering to explain this as when I've spoken to audiences across the USA, and mentioned L-plates, arms shoot up into the air to ask me what L-plates are!

Perhaps there is the need for us to wear L-plates on our backs at all times in life. After all, the learning never stops and at any moment we may, metaphorically or really, go the wrong way up a one-way street, forget to indicate or brake suddenly. It is a part of the human condition. Learning unravels itself moment by moment. The more moments where you can pay attention and notice what is happening, the more choices you have … but you know that already, right? As my daughter would say to me, 'Yeah, yeah, yeah Daddy, I heard you the last time you said it …'

> Be more of a Mood Architect and choose your best state to get the best outcome.

I love that IDENTITY statement – if I do say so myself! Be a Mood Architect: someone that takes responsibility for designing and building the most appropriate mood for that moment.

How much time do *you* spend being a Mood Architect? How often do *you* notice your mood, shape your mood and take some ACTION to adapt it if necessary?

On a scale of 0–10, how would you score yourself at your frequency of being a master of Mood Architecture? Go on be honest with yourself …

As a singer, I would often sign up for contracts that were 12 months long. Jeez. That's a hell of a long time to sign your life away for eight shows, every single week. It's relentless. On too many occasions I failed to be a good enough Mood Architect. I'm not proud of it, but fortunately those moments never lasted long before I realized something wasn't working and managed to give myself a good kick up the arse.

I sometimes found myself torn – 7.29pm and 3000 people sat in the auditorium having paid good money to see this show. I was tired and nearing the end of an already challenging day. Did I really want to drag myself around the stage for the next three hours? No. I would like to go to the pub, eat steak and drink red wine. Aaaaahhhhh … bliss. But no, 3000 people are waiting and the orchestra is starting up.

… I want steak and red wine though … but there's an audience out there…

… and I REALLY want steak, a homely pub and red wine. Do you not hear me?!

Oh, those two voices often battled in my head. They were the tough days. If my 'pub, steak and red wine' voice became the dominant one though, I was doomed, along with the other cast members and the audience of 3000!

Once or twice I succumbed to my 'pub, steak and red wine' demon and ended up rather begrudgingly mooching through the entire show. I am sorry to all the audience members that had to sit through those particular performances. If you know you were one of them, please contact the theatre box office directly for a full refund …

Seriously, it's not that clever. As always though, the Jolt eventually appeared. This time it was in the shape of a fellow cast member who decided to tell me how he felt. He came to my dressing room during the interval and politely asked if I had a minute to spare. I barely had a chance to nod and say yes, before he looked me straight in the eye and said, 'When you're on form, you're really on form and when you're not, you're a lazy s**t. This show, you're a lazy s**t!' And then he left. Jolt!

Now, I had convinced myself that it was only me who knew I was in my 'pub, steak and red wine' mood. I hadn't figured that other people might notice that too. If he picked up on it, how many of the 3000 people in the audience also noticed and, as a result, felt short changed?

Failing to be a Mood Architect can come with a hefty bill as it will see you bringing out the wrong mood at the wrong time. At some point you will pay.

During the epic film, All That Jazz, there is a recurring moment where the lead character of Joe Gideon, played by Roy Scheider, repeatedly looks in the mirror and gives himself a very clear command:

'It's show time, folks!'

This was his cue to turn it on: rise up a notch, switch on the performance, shift gears, change state and be a Mood Architect. Let the dazzle commence!

Despite my 'pub, steak and red wine' moods, the learnt ability to shift into the 'It's Showtime' zone is inherent within artists and their Artful approach. I know, I know, I hear you – I slipped off a few times. I have L-plates on which means I am in a constant loop of learning. It's ok to get it wrong providing you get the Jolt, take the learning on and then act on it.

I recently had a coaching session booked with a client for 4pm. He entered the room in a state of what can only be described as manic rage; bulging eyeballs, sweating and spitting venom. I know not everyone likes working with me, but this was ridiculous. I was quick to hold the mirror up as it felt like it was going to severely hinder the work we needed to do. He went on to tell me that his 7am meeting had really kicked his day off into a bad one. Since then he had to run conference calls, a team meeting, a senior team presentation, one-to-ones and an interview for a new team member. Right. I know what you're thinking and I was thinking the same: what footprint have you left today? How, through the mood you have chosen, have you made this organization a better place? You had a bad meeting nine hours ago and you are still carrying it around with you? You're a very senior leader, with huge amounts of influence and you spend an entire day acting in this way – really?!

Look, I appreciate stuff happens and you have to respond to it in the best way possible. Remember though, it's not what happens to you, it's what you choose to do about it!

This, however, was a classic example of the need to be more present and to be a Mood Architect. There isn't always someone around that will be brave enough to tell you that you are a lazy s**t so the requirement sits with you to notice and take action. Once you have done that, you can remind yourself that 'It's Showtime' and crank it up a notch.

Listen though, 'Showtime' does not imply Jazz hands time! Turning yourself into a song and dance show-stealer is not the mission. It is simply about giving yourself a Jolt and provoking you to choose your best mood for that occasion. This means still being authentic and truthful. It is the cue for you to check that you are bringing the best version of yourself out to play.

Whatever your role, whoever you are, whatever you have to deliver, your organization has a performance to give every single day. Your customers expect you to be able to switch on and crank it up. The question is: are you rising to the challenge?

★ Over to You

If you are already practising 'Getting turned on' and spending more time in the moment, then you will find this Jolt easier to adopt as a new habit.

You are practising it, aren't you …?!

Begin by paying attention to the moods you create. Where does your mood get you more of what you want and when does it let you down?

Which parts of your day are a bind? Where do you need to create a new mood to get new outcomes?

The repetition of 'It's Showtime' needs to sink in. You now need to play around with it and see what you conjure up. The simple fact of giving yourself this command will fire off a THINKING and ACTION upgrade.

The final Jolt: Spend your power wisely

I have a gift for you. I would like you to have £100. I know, I'm just a generous kind of guy.

Five fresh and crisp £20 notes. Here you go …

So, what will you do with it?

Buy some champagne?

Put it towards your electricity and gas bills?

Have a massage?

Take your family for a KFC family bucket?

Buy additional copies of *Jolt* and give them away as Christmas presents?

Put it into a savings account?

Buy lottery tickets?

Donate it to charity?

Invest it in shares?

Put it towards the weekly shop?

Burn it?

Seriously, take a moment to think how you would get greatest value from it ...

It's funny the responses people have when this question is focused on money. People often take great care in considering their options, as £100 is quite a chunk of extra cash to be given. It is unlikely that you will have said that you would burn it. Right? The dilemma for many will be between dealing with the here and now (pay bills, buy food ...), treating yourself (massage, champagne, KFC), putting it somewhere safe (under the mattress, in a savings account) or gambling it for a bigger pay off at some point (shares, lottery).

Where did your response fit?

Of course this book isn't offering you some extra cash. Unless you choose to auction your own copy for thousands ... No, this book merely offers you choice and greater power; power to influence, negotiate, communicate, connect, have impact and ultimately be extraordinary.

The fascinating thing here though is that once the £100 has gone, you could still get another £100 from somewhere else: work overtime, an extra job, busking, selling things on ebay, theft, car boot your comic collection ...

Spending your power also means you will be spending your energy, your time, your commitment and yourself. Once that is spent, you really won't get it back. Once they have been used up, they're gone!

Based on that, I want you now to really consider, with great care, how you will go about spending your own power.

You could spend your power on the here and now (fire fighting, going to more meetings, doing more of the same as yesterday!), treating yourself (building in some thinking time, self-reflection), putting your power somewhere safe until you need it for a rainy day (trudge along, be ordinary, tick the basic boxes) or gambling it to get a bigger pay back at some point (daring to go to your edge, asking the tougher question, inviting the uncomfortable feedforward …)?

It is no use if I tell you what you *should* do with it – you must own your decision. It's your power, not mine. Time for you to T-D-A!

Throughout *Jolt*, my role has been to prod you and shake up your thinking so that you begin to stretch more, risk more and dare more. Daring means walking closer to the edge. That of course comes with the increased risk of toppling off. However, what it also brings is excitement, learning and the possibility that you will embrace extraordinary.

Just a Jolt. Spend your power wisely. Spend it on the stuff that matters most.

The secret

I have learnt a great deal about the formula for extraordinary over the years. I have shared that with you throughout this book and I am confident that you now have more choices available to you than you did before starting to read. Some of you will be bold and take action right now and some won't … yet.

I have a secret though, and I decided to save it until the end. I have done that for a good reason.

Throughout the book, I have encouraged you to get active and test out the ideas as we go along. It's all too easy to wait until you reach the final chapter before considering your options. I wanted you to *get playful* from the outset. And that is why I kept the secret until the end. Perhaps if you heard it at the start, you would have engaged with each Jolt differently …

There are two things you need to know about your journey towards extraordinary:

1. Most of the qualities, attitudes, behaviours and processes that made you good in the first place will not be the same ones that you need in order to kiss extraordinary on the lips. Simply doing more of the same, because at some point in history it worked for you, does not provide your ticket to extraordinary. You will need to be brave enough to let much of it go so that you create the space for new habits to be installed.

And …

2. Arriving at extraordinary doesn't exist!

Shock horror. There, now I've told you. Extraordinary is ever moving, which is what makes it extraordinary in the first place! Too many people fool themselves into thinking that they have, at last, arrived. This can be dangerous. You know better than I do that the fast paced environment your business operates within requires constant upgrading to stay ahead of the game. The problem with believing that you have reached extraordinary and your place of utopia is that it very quickly renders you just ordinary again or, at best, good. I have seen many leaders believe that they have 'arrived' – however, there are those out there who continue to track down extraordinary moments and they will be the ones that ultimately have the upper hand as they zoom past those that have become complacent.

Once you have adopted these Jolts as your new story and your new habits, there is little chance that you will become complacent. Each one in its own right challenges you to keep asking the questions that will enable you to notice your choice points, decide on your THINKING and take the ACTION that transforms you from ordinary to extraordinary.

The final push …

I started off this book by clearly setting out the need for you to take action. I know you will have had no problem grasping the concepts and getting your mind wrapped around what it is you need to do to soar from ordinary to extraordinary. In so many ways, that will have been the easy part.

Armed with your new thinking, new ideas and new insights from peeping through the Artful lens, I want you now to ACT. Over many years I have observed how people with ordinary skills and ordinary talents can achieve the most extraordinary things. They do so by shaping more *enabling* beliefs than *disabling* ones. They then point their mind in the direction of travel and follow through with the appropriate action: constantly nudging forwards, 1° at a time.

No TRYING just DOING. The word *try* implies impossibility. We all need to take heed of Yoda in Star Wars. He had it bang on when he said – 'Do or do not. There is no try.' Notice the language in your outcomes and if you spot a *try* neatly tucked in there, lose it. Your extraordinary moments will be grounded in commitment and *doing*.

I wanted this book to be a catalyst for conversation. I fancied the idea of a dialogue opening up – between you and me, you and yourself, you and your team and you with your wider organization. So, I have put my views out there and for it to be a two-way thing, I need you to respond. I would love to hear how you grapple with this stuff; how you get up when you fall and how you celebrate when it all comes together. I may have opened a can of worms for you. That's ok as long as you don't eat them. Share your screw ups and your MOBs with me. Drop me a line anytime you like. I will always respond. If you fancy the idea of me coming in and chatting with your organization about how you can take on any of these Jolts and helping you get up close and personal with extraordinary, you can find me hanging out over here: richard@btfi.co.uk.

Well, the moment has arrived for your performance to move on. So as you edge closer towards extraordinary:

Dare more.

Spend more time in the room!

Upgrade. Consistently.

Seek to understand more than you ever have before.

Risk more.

Get wonky … just a little bit.

Stop sharing MOCs and hand out more MOBs …

Adopt the posture of extraordinary.

Be bold. Own yourself.

Notice the spaces in between the notes you play.

Dare to begin before you are ready.

Stop DOING leadership. Start BEING a leader.

Find your voice and let it erupt.

Unleash your more Artful self.

Be a contribution and add greater value … by just 1°.

Adopting these habits will be your springboard towards extraordinary. Sitting around and pondering them will not create changes. Shaking up your THINKING and taking ACTION, will!

And remember …

Stuff happens all the time. Things will fly your way and occasionally things will pull the rug from under your feet. It's called life. It's not about that though; it's what you choose to do about it that really counts.

I want to leave you with the beautiful and inspiring words of David McNally from his book, *Even Eagles Need a Push*.

> *The eagle gently coaxed her offspring toward the edge of the nest, her heart quivered with conflicting emotions as she felt their resistance to her persistent nudging.*
>
> *Why does the thrill of soaring have to begin with the fear of falling she thought? The ageless question was still unanswered for her. As in the tradition of the species her nest was located high upon the shelf of a sheer rock face. Below there was nothing but air to support the wings of each child.*
>
> *Is it possible that this time it will not work she thought …*
>
> *Despite her fears the eagle knew it was time her parental mission was all but complete and there remained one final task. THE PUSH.*
>
> *The eagle drew courage from an innate wisdom. Until her children discovered their wings, there was no purpose for their lives. Until they learned how to soar they would fail to understand the privilege it was to have been born an eagle. The push was the greatest gift she had to offer. It was her supreme act of love.*
>
> *And so, one by one she pushed them. And they FLEW*

Now it's time for you to soar too …

About Richard Tyler

Image reproduced with permission of Jack Alexander

Before setting up BTFI, Richard could be found pimping his voice in theatres and concert halls across the globe. From the two men and their whippet in a Scottish working men's club to 17,000 people at V Festival right through to leading the way in London's Phantom of the Opera, Richard carved out a successful career as a performer.

Having decided to hang up his g-string for good, he spent three years at a leading L&D consultancy before making the leap to launch BTFI. During the last 10 years, Richard and his team have been pioneers of Artful Leadership – bringing jazz, music, theatre and performance to the world of leadership, organizational development and cultural change.

Richard now spends his time as Chief Possibility Architect and provocateur, daring clients around the globe to make the shift from ordinary to extraordinary. He is in demand as a coach, keynote speaker and facilitator. Richard writes for various trade journals and frequently speaks on radio.

Apart from appearing in a prime time TV commercial along with a dog (never again!) Richard is still hopeful that his ambition to appear in a BBC costume drama will at some point be realized …

Acknowledgements

Jolt existed in my head for many years before I finally felt brave enough to get it down on paper. It is the result of 42 years worth of work! That journey would not have been possible without the support of some significant people along the way.

Firstly to the extraordinary team at Capstone (Wiley) for helping make this book a reality. Thank you for believing in me and seeing a glimmer of magic in *Jolt*. Your persistent energy and encouragement is remarkable.

To Mr Lewis and Mrs Instone for daring me to be bold and to follow my dream. At 12-years-old, you were the teachers that gave me a Jolt and inspired me to go BTFI. Thank you for presenting me with so many opportunities that paved the way ahead.

To my mum and dad for all those hours and hours of waiting for me when I had tap dancing lessons and rehearsals. Sorry my dancing never improved! Dad, I am sure you would have described this book as a 'jolly good effort!'

To my many wonderful clients who have taught me so much and have contributed to *Jolt*. Thank you for taking on all my tough love and stretching yourselves to extraordinary.

To the team at Timberyard, Seven Dials that make London's best coffee and sell the most awesome cakes. Thank you for keeping me fed and caffeinated during much of my writing!

To the team at BTFI, especially the stonkingly talented Sara Colman and Al Gurr. I am blessed to have you on board. Your skill, attitude and insight are true gifts.

To Petra, thank you for continuing to hound me to write this thing. It only took five years!

To my Mia, you will never know how much you inspire me. Your constant chatter, singing, dancing and 'Derren Brown' mind games remain my greatest source of inspiration. Thank you for checking in, every single day, as to how many words I had written! Keep being extraordinary. I love you lots.

Index